From Rigorous Standards to Student Achievement

A Practical Process

Michael D. Rettig

Laura L. McCullough

Karen E. Santos

Charles R. Watson

EYE ON EDUCATION

EYE ON EDUCATION
6 DEPOT WAY WEST, SUITE 106
LARCHMONT, NY 10538
(914) 833–0551
(914) 833–0761 fax
www.eyeoneducation.com

Library of Congress Cataloging-in-Publication Data

From rigorous standards to student achievement : a practical process / Michael D. Rettig ... [et al.]
   p. cm.
  ISBN 1-9305556-62-4
    1. Education–Standards–United States. Academic achievement–United States. 3. Educational accountability–United States. I. Rettig, Michael D., 1950–.

LB3060.83.F76   2003
379.I′58–dc21

                                     2003053161

10 9 8 7 6 5 4 3 2 1

Editorial and production services provided by
Richard H. Adin Freelance Editorial Services
52 Oakwood Blvd., Poughkeepsie, NY 12603-4112
(845-471-3566)

Also Available from EYE ON EDUCATION

Achievement Now!
How to Assure No Child Is Left Behind
Dr. Donald J. Fielder

The Principal as Instructional Leader:
A Handbook for Supervisors
Sally J. Zepeda

Navigating Comprehensive School Change:
A Guide for the Perplexed
Thomas G. Chenoweth and Robert B. Everhart

Differentiated Instruction:
A Guide for Elementary School Teachers
Amy Benjamin

Differentiated Instruction:
A Guide for Middle and High School Teachers
Amy Benjamin

Handbook on Teacher Evaluation:
Assessing and Improving Performance
James H. Stronge and Pamela D. Tucker

Handbook on Educational Specialist Evaluation:
Assessing and Improving Performance
James H. Stronge and Pamela D. Tucker

What Great Teachers Do Differently:
14 Things That Matter Most
Todd Whitaker

What Great Principals Do Differently:
15 Things That Matter Most
Todd Whitaker

Real Teachers, Real Challenges, Real Solutions:
25 Ways to Handle the Challenges of the Classroom Effectively
Annette and Elizabeth Breaux

Dedication

This book is dedicated to our families, who tolerate
our passion for our work and forgive us for our absences.

About the Authors

Michael D. Rettig currently is professor in the School of Education and Director of the Center for School Leadership at James Madison University in Harrisonburg, Virginia. He taught public school for 10 years in the Syracuse City Schools in New York and has served as an elementary and middle school administrator in two Virginia school districts.

During the past decade Mike has conducted workshops and seminars on the topics of school scheduling, strategies for engaging active learners, and curriculum pacing at more than 50 national and state conferences. In addition, he has served as a consultant with more than 500 school districts in 35 states. He is co-author of four books and more than a dozen journal articles.

Mike earned a Ph.D. in Educational Leadership and Policy Studies from the University of Virginia, a M.Ed. from S.U.N.Y. at Cortland, and a B.S. from Syracuse University. He was named a University Scholar in 1972 by Syracuse University and was the recipient of the Phi Delta Kappa outstanding graduate student award in 1991 at the University of Virginia. In March 1999, Mike was named a Madison Scholar at James Madison University. He and his wife, Sally, have a son, Dan, and two daughters, Anne and Alison.

Laura L. McCullough has taught at the elementary, middle, high school, undergraduate, and graduate levels. She has also served as a math/science coordinator, staff development specialist, and elementary principal. Laura is currently the Director of Instruction for Waynesboro Public Schools in Virginia.

Laura received a B.S. Ed. from Longwood College, and a M.Ed. and Ed.D. in Curriculum and Instruction from the University of Virginia. She teaches as adjunct faculty at James Madison University and at the University of Virginia. She provides staff development in the areas of curriculum planning, student assessment, math instruction, school improvement planning, and cognitive coaching.

Karen E. Santos is a professor of education and serves as the coordinator of the special education teacher preparation program at James Madison University in Harrisonburg, Virginia. She has taught students with disabilities in Virginia, served as an educational diagnostician, curriculum specialist, and a school district coordinator of special education services.

Karen received a B.S. degree in Communication Disorders and Deaf Education from Northwestern University, and M.Ed. and Ph.D. in Special Education from the University of Virginia. She was named the outstanding teacher at James Madison University and received the Carl Harter Distinguished Teaching Award in 1998. She received the JMU Madison Scholar award in 2002 and Provost Award for Excellence in 2003.

Karen provides numerous state and national workshops for teachers and administrators in the areas of differentiation of instruction, curriculum access, and inclusionary practices for working with students with special needs. She has presented more than 40 sessions at national conferences in the last five years. She is co-author of a case teaching book and seven journal articles. A federal Student Initiated Research grant was awarded to support doctoral research. Karen resides in Staunton, Virginia with her husband, Victor, and they have two sons, Brandon and Carter.

Charles R. Watson has been involved in teaching, education and school improvement for more than 30 years. He has been a middle school math and science teacher, an administrator, and is currently a Professor of Education at the University of Evansville and Chair of the School of Education. He teaches courses in science education and methods, middle schools, teacher leadership, and assessment. His areas of expertise and research are middle level education, science education, curriculum alignment and integration, educational reform and improvement, parent involvement in schools, rural education, and school leadership. He has worked with schools and teams of teachers and administrators in the areas of middle level education and school improvement in many states, especially throughout the Appalachian area and the eastern United States. He has published in the area of instructional practice, curriculum models, and curriculum alignment and improvement. He holds degrees in Business Administration, School Counseling, and a doctorate in Educational Leadership.

Table of Contents

Preface

Educators have met the implementation of high academic standards across the country with varied levels of resistance and denial. When first confronted with the fact that students will be tested and schools will be evaluated based upon students' performance, principals and teachers often respond with shock, disbelief, and denial. "This too shall pass" is a common refrain. With mounting evidence that the new accountability system actually will be implemented, a sense of awareness develops that often is troubling and overwhelming. The challenge of helping all students meet difficult learning standards causes anger, guilt, and frustration: "How can we do that?" With the reauthorization of the Elementary and Secondary Education Act (ESEA) and the "No Child Left Behind" federal legislation in 2002, the challenge to help more students attain higher academic standards has intensified. At some point, perhaps not until the first results are printed in the local newspaper, the principal and teachersddo move beyond denial and begin the search for practical ways to improve students' achievement. We believe that this search offers an opportunity for renewal. It is to that purpose that this book is dedicated.

Our central belief in this book is that there must be a constant tension between two somewhat conflicting goals: the attainment of high academic standards by all students and the provision of a developmentally appropriate learning environment. Placing too much emphasis on students achieving high standards causes disengagement, burnout, and disillusionment among students and teachers. When schools become obsessed with the idea that all students must achieve the same standards, they often fail to recognize that this can only be accomplished through a flexible and highly differentiated instructional program that offers students more than one way to learn. Similarly, when schools overemphasize developmental appropriateness, they often neglect to provide students with clear and sufficiently challenging expectations related to content. Our charge as educators is to find the appropriate balance.

We do not propose any one instructional strategy or program as a panacea for student achievement deficits; no such program exists. There are, however, many research-supported instructional approaches and curricula that are worthy of consideration. We encourage schools to seek out such strategies. Instead, we propose schoolwide processes for planning curriculum delivery, assessing student learning, monitoring group and individual progress, and developing instructional interventions.

In this book we build on the work of Heidi Hayes-Jacobs (1997) and Fenwick English (1980) by answering the question: What do we do once our curriculum is aligned? We describe a process of curriculum implementation that includes four interwoven strands:

1. The design and use of curriculum "pacing guides"

2. The design and use of formative assessments

3. The periodic review of students' progress and the adjustment of instruction and pacing by a collaborative group in "staffing meetings"

4. The planning and use of modified instructional activities

Implicit in these processes are the following four beliefs:

- ♦ The responsibility for student achievement and instructional quality resides at the school level. Consequently, we also believe that

- ♦ Schools should be held accountable for students' achievement.

- ♦ School improvement must be school-based.

- ♦ Teachers should make decisions regarding curriculum pacing and sequencing collaboratively even though curriculum design and curriculum alignment may be district-level functions.

These responsibilities belong to the school staff as a whole; they cannot be divided among individuals. Consequently, we also believe that

- ♦ Goal-focused collaboration is essential.

- ♦ Goal-focused collaboration is a powerful staff development activity.

- ♦ Periodic review of group and individual progress by the collaborative teaching team is a critical aspect of the school improvement process.

- ♦ Instructional interventions are more easily provided within the context of a supportive collaborative teaching team and a school organizational structure that has been designed to respond proactively when students don't learn.

To plan and make decisions in a goal-focused, collaborative manner, teachers need a systematic school improvement process that is informed by multiple data sources. Thus, we also believe that

- ♦ What gets monitored gets done.

- ♦ Reporting of students' achievement on state summative assessments rarely provides enough specific data on which to plan school improvement efforts.

- Formative assessment of students' progress is necessary to provide specific data for the improvement of students' achievement.

- School-based formative assessment efforts should use multiple data sources.

- Assessments of students' learning should only be conducted as frequently as educators are willing to make changes in instruction.

Students learn at different rates and in different ways. Consequently, we also believe that

- The decisions made in schools should be driven primarily by careful consideration of student needs.

- Students' learning needs should be identified and accommodated prior to and during the delivery of instruction.

- The amount of learning (for most students) should be a constant (or standard); the time it takes to learn should be the variable.

The process we describe is logical, practical, and supported by research (Marzano, 2000; English, 1980). We believe it provides a structure which supports teachers and principals in "raising the bar" for students, while effectively meeting the needs of diverse learners.

Acknowledgments

The authors acknowledge the hundreds of teachers and principals who taught us what we know about the work described in these pages. Their students are blessed with the finest of teachers and leaders. In particular, we are indebted to the faculties and leadership in Waynesboro City, Lexington City, Madison County, and Orange County, Virginia; as well as the teachers at Stone-Robinson Elementary School. Thanks to Erin King, graduate student at James Madison University, for her research and help in reformatting many of the visuals in the text. We are also grateful to Bev Winter of Waynesboro, Virginia Public Schools for expert clerical support.

1

Introduction and Overview

Many factors influence instructional decisions about curriculum, teaching, and learning. Satisfying what looks to be an ever-increasing number of educational and political demands can overwhelm teachers, principals, and others involved in the education of children. "Higher standards" and test scores have become the clear winners in the battle to find ways to make schools and educational systems accountable to the public.

Nearly all states and many school districts use a variety of tests and standards to demonstrate levels of student achievement, and many states currently attach financial rewards as well as financial penalties to student test results. Some use test results as the basis for accreditation, and nearly every state has recently "raised the bar" for students' achievement. The pressures associated with these actions are enormous. How do educators respond? Consider these three scenarios:

School Principal

This summer, I ran around the state to every possible workshop and presentation that related to the federal regulations, state standards, and increasing student achievement. My office is overflowing with test data, results of analyses, presentation handouts, and the latest books. The central office made it quite clear that in comparison to state averages, our test scores in the school district as a whole and in my school in particular must rise significantly this year. I remember how frustrated I felt when I saw that several of our scores in two grade levels even dropped below last year's scores. This year, in addition to lots of other projects and programs, the central office administrators are providing district-wide workshops conducted by consultants from the local university to target curriculum areas that are especially problematic. If they send me one more announcement or set of guidelines, I think I'll scream! I've tried to incorporate many of these initiatives into my school goals and plans for staff development this year, but the bottom line is, we need to improve test scores, and I am not sure where to focus the limited time that is available. Pockets of teachers are trying new things and are energized by the challenge, but there are others in my building who are clearly unwilling to change how they've always done things despite a new curriculum and significantly increased accountability. They don't seem to believe this is really happening. How am I going to be able to get them to support each other, motivate them to try new methods, and encourage them to share across grade levels and disciplines so that ultimately the students are the ones who gain? Parents cannot be ignored in this process either, and that's no small task. I just cannot bear to think of the consequences of another year of poor test results published in the local newspaper. It is my responsibility to turn things around, but where should I start?

This vignette is representative of situations taking place all across the country. Principals are asking:

- ◆ Where do I start?
- ◆ How will I convince my teachers that this is important and, unlike many circumstances in the past, won't go away?
- ◆ What steps do I take now?
- ◆ How do I monitor our progress?
- ◆ Where will I get the resources to put together a realistic program?
- ◆ How do I get help from the central office?
- ◆ What kind of help do I need?
- ◆ What do I tell the parents?
- ◆ What will I do about the teachers who might actively resist doing anything?
- ◆ Where will I get the time to do this?

Central Office Administrator

Planning the summer administrative retreat has been a real challenge because we need to accomplish so many things in such a short time. The school board has made it abundantly clear how they feel about our relative ranking in the state based on assessment results. Certainly, the curriculum standards must be a main area of focus, but issues like school violence and teacher shortages cannot be ignored.

Building principals need to be brought on board in terms of district-wide test score improvement, and yet we must be very careful about creating undue competitiveness between schools in the district. It is especially hard for those schools with increased numbers of at-risk students. And now "No Child Left Behind" requires us to show adequate yearly progress (AYP) for our lowest performing students. We want the teachers and principals to feel like they have our support as they attempt to raise local test scores, but the areas of need are so diverse that it is difficult to provide staff development that satisfies everyone.

Central Office administrators are asking:

- How can I meet the demands of the school board in the midst of this complexity?

- How do I figure out what staff development activities to support and plan?

- How do I convince principals and teachers that we will support them?

- How do I use the curriculum specialists to help the schools?

- What resources am I going to need?

- How do I pay attention to test scores and still give other problem areas the attention they need?

- Where can I get more information about subject matter?

- How do I get information and resources to teachers and principals?

- What do I do about principals who may not be truly committed to the process?

Teacher

I'm going to cry if one more person tells me something else to do to raise my test scores. They don't seem to understand that I have more students with special needs than other teachers. How am I supposed to get all these kids to pass the state assessments? Some of them can barely read, and I doubt they will ever learn all this material. Every faculty meeting, memo, and announcement emphasizes a new program or strategy. How can I possibly do all of these things and still cover the content? Not only are these students under too much pressure, but also I'm tired of focusing solely on these standards. I used to develop creative interdisciplinary lessons that incorporated art and music activities but now it is just memorization, memorization, memorization. . . . It's just too much for the kids and I'm beginning to think it's too much for me. I'm tired of being on the firing line.

Because of extensive media attention to test scores and comparative rankings, teachers often are forced to ask:

- Is this just another one of many educational reforms I've experienced in my career, or is this focus on tests and scores here to stay?

- How many of these so-called reforms will I have to endure?

- How can I do what I think I need to do with my students and still meet these test score pressures?

- These "standards" are all either too broad and unspecified, or they are just sets of things to memorize. How can I sort all of this out?

- Will I have to give up all of the successful curriculum units I've developed over the years?

- How can I explain all this to my students' parents?

- What will happen to the students who do not pass the state tests?

- If my kids don't do well on these tests, could I lose my job?

Teachers often feel that they have little power with respect to their positions or their profession, yet the focus on standards and the many comparisons that are made in the media often keep teachers and principals at the center of the attention. Moreover, given the ever-increasing demands on teachers' time and energy, it is easy to understand how teachers can feel powerless. We believe that the processes we describe in this book can help teachers regain some control over their professional lives.

The emphasis on higher standards and test scores has had a profound impact on how educators view curriculum. Specifically, it has underscored the importance of "mapping" and "aligning" the curriculum with assessments and testing processes. Consequently, we currently see very few schools or districts that have not embarked on the difficult but important process of aligning the curriculum with assessments and standards. Unfortunately, meeting the challenge of high standards and improving achievement does not stop with an aligned curriculum. Often schools undergo a thorough curriculum mapping and alignment process only to find that few teachers actually use the documents created to change or inform classroom practices. When this happens, the time-consuming process of curriculum alignment becomes just another bureaucratic paper chase.

We feel strongly that the mapping and alignment process is extremely important. However, we are certain that it is even more important for schools and teachers to take the next logical step and use the aligned curriculum to guide and inform instructional and assessment decisions. Marzano's (2000) meta-analysis of school improvement research lends strong support to our assertion. The variable "opportunity to learn" was the single most important school factor influencing students' achievement. Opportunity to learn was defined as, "the extent to which a school (1) has a well-articulated curriculum, (2) addresses the content in those assessments used to make judgments about student achievement, and (3) monitors the extent to which teachers actually cover the articulated curriculum" (p. 48).

This is the substance of our book, how to guarantee a viable curriculum (Marzano, 2003). The activities detailed in each chapter are designed as the next logical steps following the critical initial mapping and alignment of curriculum. The collaborative processes described ensure that curriculum and instruction are sequenced and paced appropriately, assessed regularly, and adjusted as needed. These practical activities have assisted many schools in successfully meeting the challenge of improving student achievement and meeting high standards.

A Model for School Improvement

The improvement model illustrated in Figure 1.1 depicts the process in more detail. The *curriculum plan*, as indicated in the upper left portion of the figure, represents the mapped, aligned, and paced curriculum. That is, the curriculum plan is the document or set of documents that results from mapping out the present curriculum, as it exists, aligning it with standards or assessments, and creating calendar-based pacing guides.[1] Our work and this book begin with the creation of the pacing guides, two- or three-page documents that outline on a calendar the objectives included in instructional units, and the sequence and duration of these units. It is possible and relatively time efficient to begin the process here, even if a district or school-level aligned curriculum does not exist. Just use the state-mandated objectives (e.g., *The Standards of Learning in Virginia*) as the aligned curriculum. Many smaller school districts create pacing guides directly from these documents.

---

1 The terms *curriculum mapping, curriculum alignment*, and *curriculum pacing* are often used interchangeably. We see them as parts of a larger effort, and so we define curriculum mapping as a process by which the existing curriculum is described and recorded on a curriculum map. Curriculum alignment is the process of adjusting the mapped curriculum to match a set of standards, typically ones mandated by the state. "Curriculum pacing" entails sequencing the realigned curriculum, allocating time to the various units, and placing this plan on a calendar.

Figure 1.1 Improvement Model

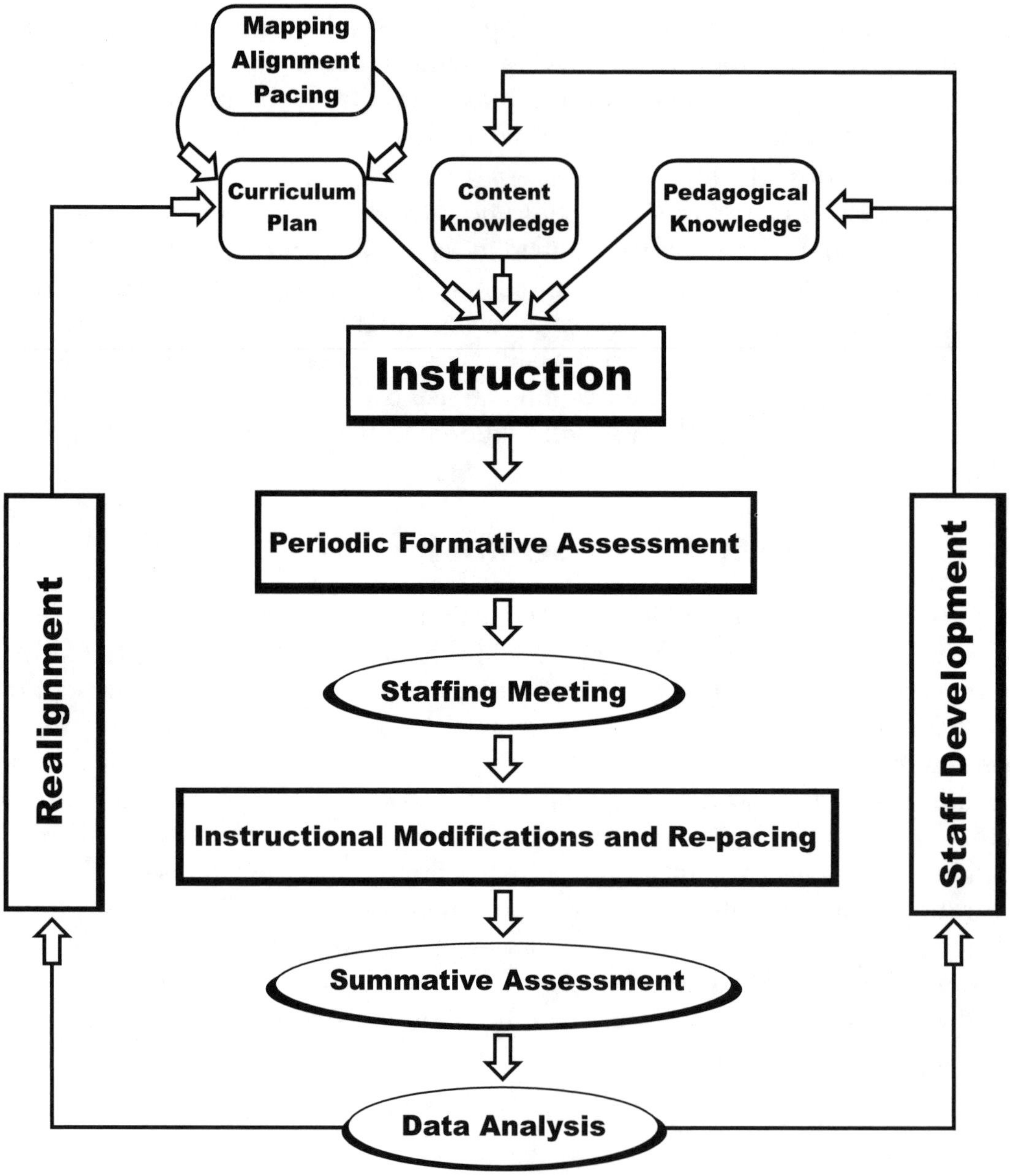

The aligned curriculum provides the basis for developing pacing guides that help teachers plan instruction, design instructional units, assign time-frames to lessons and units, and bring the curriculum to life. A school or school district may have a beautifully aligned and thoroughly detailed curriculum plan, but unless the plan is used and becomes part of a living support system for teachers, it is meaningless. Chapter 2 presents a set of practical strategies for creating *pacing guides*—and pacing guides, in our opinion and experience, are the heart of this process.

Armed with a collaboratively designed *curriculum plan*, teachers with sound *content knowledge* and appropriate *pedagogical knowledge* will be well prepared for *instruction*. Content knowledge and pedagogical knowledge are mentioned only slightly in this book, however; we must stress that these two areas are extremely important. Content knowledge is crucial; teachers will be unable to make good decisions regarding pacing, assessment, or instruction unless their knowledge of content is sound and deep. Likewise, pedagogical knowledge is extremely important; teachers need to take their deep knowledge of content and through effective instruction make the curriculum come alive.

If pacing guides are the heart of the process, *assessment* is the brain. Once decisions have been made regarding the teaching of content or skills, frequent, meaningful, and responsive assessment is critical for success. *Periodic formative assessment* informs instructional decision making. Chapter 3 describes a number of useful and practical assessment strategies and actions that help teachers make informed decisions about student learning.

Chapter 4 describes a process we call *staffings.* A staffing is a periodically scheduled, structured meeting that provides a mechanism for teachers and principals to monitor student learning, make adjustments, and plan instructional interventions. We know that even the best instructional plans can go awry or take much longer than anticipated; staffings provide regular opportunities to monitor and measure ourselves as well as our students. Using data from *formative assessments* and the collective wisdom of the professionals in attendance, teams may decide to *re-pace* curriculum, offer extra help for an individual or small groups of students, or perhaps attempt other *instructional modifications.* We know that not all students learn at the same pace or in the same manner, and indeed, there are many students who may not be able or inclined to keep up with what the pacing guides suggest.

Chapter 5 illustrates a problem-solving strategy called the IEP-DR for designing *instruction* to accommodate the needs of learners.

Once the *summative assessment*, most probably the state-mandated high stakes test, has been administered, and results are returned and *data analyzed*, the entire process and system must be carefully examined to help identify and plan *staff development* activities, provide additional training and skills development, and perhaps engage in a *realignment* of the curriculum plan.

The processes we describe in this book are not easy or simple; indeed, even at the level of the individual classroom, the tasks are complex and need to be well organized and supported. With persistence and careful follow-through, however, the steps we prescribe will be effective in improving student outcomes. Chapter 6 provides ideas and strategies to assist leaders who are responsible for supporting and guiding the process at the district and school levels.

2

Creating Pacing Guides: The Curriculum Component

The first step in a school's plan to improve student achievement is the creation of pacing guides. A pacing guide is simply a standardized format for planning when and for how long objectives in a curriculum will be taught. The process of creating the pacing guide includes three elements: (1) learning objectives are grouped into units, (2) time is allocated to each of the units, and (3) the units are sequenced onto a calendar. When teachers actually create pacing guides, they simultaneously think about emphasis (time allocation) and sequence. Without a pacing guide we will not have a plan to ensure that our curriculum will be taught prior to the administration of a summative assessment. With a pacing guide we have at least planned a means for covering all material.

Many educators would argue that course-pacing guides have been available for years, having been created for teachers by committees as a routine part of the curriculum development process. Some states (e.g., North Carolina) also have produced pacing guides for courses in which there are statewide end-of-course examinations. The questions are, however, are these documents practical, and are they actually used? It has been our experience from years of participation on such committees that the *writers* of curriculum and pacing guides do use the documents and do develop a deep understanding of the curriculum they are to teach. The problem is that curriculum writing is often the province of a select group of individuals who are organized into district-wide committees. Do other teachers, who have not been involved in the writing process, actually use the curriculum and pacing guide? Our experience tells us implementation at the classroom level is spotty at best. Thus, our goal when writing pacing guides is not just the creation of the documents themselves; our goal is for *all teachers* who teach in a particular curriculum area *to learn the curriculum* and *to formulate a plan for its instruction*. The pacing guide is a vehicle that structures this learning.

Although the basic steps of creating a pacing guide are not difficult, we find the process and discussion in which teachers engage to create the guides to be very sophisticated and healthy. Teachers bring their opinions regarding sequencing, unit emphasis, integration, and review strategies to the discussions. They negotiate from their positions and almost always create a pacing guide that is more carefully thought out than any individual teacher's effort. This process is exciting to participate in and to observe. Any principal or department chair engaged in this process soon comes to believe that this is what "instructional leadership" means.

In this chapter, we will detail a process for creating pacing guides at the school level. We answer the following questions:

- *What* is a pacing guide?
  - What formats are available?
  - What level of detail is necessary?
  - For what subjects should pacing guides be created?
- *Who* should be involved in the process of creating pacing guides?
  - Is this a core subject activity only?
  - What are the roles of special education personnel?
  - How are other specialists involved?
- *Where* and *when* are pacing guides created?
- *How* is the process managed?

What is a Pacing Guide?

As previously defined, a pacing guide is a written planning document (typically a chart) that delineates when objectives in a curriculum will be taught. The audience for the pacing guide is predominantly made up of teachers; however, pacing guides often are reformatted to be shared with parents and students. Pacing guides can vary greatly in terms of the level of detail that is included. The time available to create the pacing guide often determines the level of detail. For example, one of us has had the luxury of working for a full week with a small school system to create pacing guides in all curriculum areas. All teachers and administrators in the district were involved in the process. A high degree of detail was possible in this project. Often much less time is available to write the guides.

In its most basic form, a pacing guide includes objectives to be taught, a brief description of units created from these objectives, a time frame for the instruction of the units, and some implementation notes. The form shown in Figure 2.1

illustrates typical column headings for the *curriculum component* of a pacing guide. This format often is a good starting place for the development of this tool. Pacing guides can become much more complex; therefore, after detailing the design of the basic guide, we discuss the *assessment component* and the *instructional component*. When teachers collaborate on all three components of pacing guide development, they will engage in a process that prepares them to deliver curriculum through effective and appropriate instruction.

Pacing Guides: The Curriculum Component

Many issues arise when discussing the creation of units. We could conceivably give teachers a checklist of issues to be addressed during the production of the draft guides. From our experience we believe that this approach is inappropriate. Teachers presented with a long list of objectives, a long list of issues to consider, and a sheaf of blank pacing charts often become overwhelmed and discouraged with the task at hand. Teachers presented with only a list of objectives, blank pacing charts, and the challenge to "do the best that you can in an hour or so" will surprise themselves with the quality of their work. Invariably their discussions will address almost all of the issues of importance. Figure 2.2 (p. 13) lists what we have determined to be the major issues regarding the construction of pacing guides; there are undoubtedly others. This list could be used after the construction of first drafts. Teachers will quickly check through commenting, "Yes, we discussed this. Yes, we discussed that."

We now include a brief discussion of several of the issues listed in Figure 2.2. Although we treat "objectives and units" separately from "time frame" and "implementation notes," this is somewhat artificial. Any discussion of unit design includes a discussion of how long the unit will take to teach.

Objectives and Units

We suggest that teachers begin their discussion with the objectives. Consequently, it must be decided what objectives are to be included on the pacing guide. Figure 2.3 (p. 14) suggests potential sources of objectives; any of the objectives on this chart could be included on the pacing guide. The question becomes one of focus versus breadth. In some schools it may be appropriate to include on the pacing guide only those objectives that will be assessed on the high stakes accountability test. When students' graduation and/or school accreditation are dependent on performance on state examinations, it is understandable that some schools focus their efforts squarely on accomplishing these specific goals. Thus, if graduation for a large number of students or school accreditation is at stake, perhaps only the tested state objectives will be referenced on the pacing guide. In many school districts a curriculum guide has been developed that includes district objectives in addition to the state-level objectives. Some school

Figure 2.1. Pacing Guide (Curriculum Component)

Subject/Grade Level _____   Year _____   Authors _____   Page# _____

Time Frame	Unit Titles/Content	Objectives to Be Included	Page#

Figure 2.2. Considerations When Creating Pacing Guides

- For which subjects should pacing guides be constructed?
- Who should be involved in the design of pacing guides?
- Who is the audience for the pacing guides?
- How does the school's philosophy affect the development of pacing guides?
- What objectives must/should be taught? Are there multiple sources of objectives?
- What units should be taught?
- Could some units be interdisciplinary (covering objectives in different disciplines)?
- What objectives should be included in each unit?
- What objectives that can be "infused" throughout all units?
- When is the test?
- What baseline data is available on students?
- How much time can be allotted to teach each unit?
- What is the emphasis in the test on each objective or strand of objectives (VA SOL Testing Blueprints)?
- In what order should the units be taught?
- How can previously taught objectives be reviewed within current units?
- What objectives should be "fresh" in students' minds when the test is taken?
- Should review time be provided prior to the test?
- What accommodations should be made for the slow learner or the gifted student?
- Should (or how should) the work of creating pacing guides be divided?
- Who will review pacing guides?
- Who will receive pacing guides?

Figure 2.3. Sources of Objectives

1. Objectives from National Curriculum Sources (e.g., National Council of Teachers of Mathematics)
2. Tested state objectives
3. Tested county/city/district objectives
4. Other state objectives
5. Other county/city/district objectives
6. School objectives
7. Grade-level/department objectives
8. Teacher objectives

---

districts have developed their own district-wide examinations; there is strong motivation to include these objectives on the guide. Although still important and still taught, other district, school, and teacher objectives, for which a school is not held accountable, may or may not be included in the pacing guide. Once the source of objectives is decided, they must be grouped into units.

The grouping of objectives into units is usually a fairly obvious task; state and district curricula often include "strands" that lend themselves to unit construction. One issue that arises is how to handle objectives that cut across many strands and must be infused into several units. An example of this occurs in relation to scientific processes or scientific method, a common strand found in most science curricula. Should a separate unit be taught on these processes, or should the objectives related to the scientific method be *infused* into all units? Should both occur?

A second issue that must be addressed is *emphasis*. How much time do we spend on each of the units? A number of factors may be considered when addressing this issue. From past experience teachers generally know how long it takes to instruct certain objectives or units. Novice teachers or teachers who have not taught the curriculum previously have difficulty predicting the appropriate time frames. Dialogue with experienced teachers is helpful in these situations. Data from students' past performance on summative assessments should be analyzed to determine if there is a need to emphasize one strand of objectives over another. In some states, departments of education have produced "testing blueprints," which detail the number of test items devoted to each strand of the curriculum in a particular grade level and discipline. These documents provide another means for determining emphasis.

Another issue, which arises quite often with primary teachers, is the fact that most of the units that they teach are interdisciplinary. It makes little sense for K–2 teachers to design discipline-specific pacing guides. The pacing guide shown in Figure 2.4 allows teachers to specify a unit that covers objectives from a variety of disciplines. All teachers may find this format useful when designing interdisciplinary units.

The pacing guide should not end with the administration of the summative assessment. Because the testing window is sometimes scheduled weeks or even months prior to the end of the school year, teaching units should be designed for instruction after the summative assessments are completed. The time after the test and before the end of the school may be lost if we do not plan carefully. This time can be used for enrichment and/or remediation, based on a solid assessment of students' needs.

Time Frame

In grade levels, subjects, and/or courses with district or state tests, it is necessary to plan backward from the testing date. The first step of this process is to determine how many instructional days actually are available. To calculate this number you must subtract the number of school days that occur at the end of the year after the administration of the test, time lost because of other mandated testing, and time lost because of interruptions such as school assemblies, special programs, field trips, and the like. One superintendent calculated that in his district only 135 days of instruction were available from the 180-day calendar prior to the administration of the state assessments. We hope this is a worst-case scenario. Regardless, once the number of available days is known, teachers must apportion them to the units that have been constructed.

Teachers use a variety of formats to denote the assigned time periods. Primary teachers often plan by month, sequentially listing the months of the school year in the left column of Figure 2.1 (p. 12) (e.g., "September," "October," "November," etc.). Other teachers plan by grading periods, and thus they write "1st nine weeks," "2nd nine weeks," and so forth, in the time frame column. One high school math teacher with whom we have worked calculated the available number of teaching "blocks" (90 minutes each block for his school) in the calendar and then assigned "5 blocks" to this unit and "7 blocks" to that unit. Other teachers denote the time frame by specifying calendar dates, and then in parentheses they denote the number of teaching days, such as "September 22 to October 4 (10 days)." We prefer more specificity rather than less specificity in this planning phase. We realize, however, that the time frame denoted is an estimate and may need to be revised throughout the year.

Figure 2.4. Pacing Guide (Curriculum Component: Interdisciplinary Curriculum Pacing)

Subject/Grade Level _____   Year _____   Authors _____   Page# _____

| Time Frame | Unit Titles/Content | Objectives to Be Included | | | | Implementation Notes |
		LA/R	Math	SS	SC	

There is another key issue related to timing that must be addressed. In some grade levels and/or content areas, students may be grouped by ability or achievement level. For example, second grade teachers may regroup their students during math time, or a high school may have three different levels of ninth grade English. It is obvious that in these situations, each group will learn at a different pace. After all, this was the primary justification for grouping students in the first place. Where students are grouped in this manner, teachers often ask if there should be a unique pacing guide for each group. If so, they wonder, is it really necessary for us to get together to plan? Shouldn't we each just do our own pacing guides?

These teachers have a unique challenge when it comes to developing pacing guides and working together in staffing meetings. Most schools assert that, when they use ability grouping, these groups are "flexible," and that movement from one group to another is accommodated as students progress at different rates. If this goal is to be realized, then it is essential that teachers work together so that students have "points of entry" where they can move in and out of groups as their instructional needs dictate. Each teacher would indeed have his or her own adaptation of a basic pacing guide that the team had developed together. The fact remains, however, that state assessments have not been designed for these different groups; all students are expected to achieve up to a specified standard. Consequently, the basic pacing guide may be very similar for all levels to ensure that all students are exposed to same basic curriculum. Units for different levels could be of the same length but of varying degrees of depth. Another approach would be for more advanced groups to complete a unit in less time and then engage in a mini-unit for enrichment. This faster-paced group would then rejoin the slower group at the beginning of the next basic unit. This approach would permit the movement of students among groups at the beginning of a new unit as their performance indicated.

Implementation Notes

This category in the pacing guide simply offers teachers the opportunity to remind themselves of some key details related to the instruction of particular units. For example, in fifth grade science it is not unusual to have one electricity kit available for the entire grade level. It would be impossible, therefore, for all three or four teachers to instruct this material at the same time. Thus, in the "Implementation Notes" column it would be appropriate to delineate the rotating schedule devised for sharing these materials. In a high school U.S. history class teachers might specify a special field trip, guest speaker, or film and would use this section as a reminder to make the necessary arrangements.

Pacing Guides: The Assessment Component

Completing the *curriculum component* of pacing guides in all areas of instruction in a school is a major accomplishment and should be celebrated. Each course now has a long-range plan to ensure that the required instructional objectives are covered. The question then becomes: "Did our students learn the material we covered?" To be able to adjust instruction appropriately teachers need data regarding students' performance; they cannot wait until the results of the end-of-course or end-of-year assessments are received. Consequently, we recommend that the *assessment component* of pacing guide development be devoted to the planning of periodic assessments that are used to measure students' mastery of the taught curriculum. Discussing these results in staffing meetings should lead to appropriate modifications in instructional approach, grouping, and/or pacing. The development of these assessments is addressed in greater detail in Chapter 3. Figure 2.5 suggests one format for thinking about this design; we extend the pacing guide by adding columns entitled "Mid-Unit Assessments" and "End-Unit Assessments."

Pacing Guides: The Instructional Component

Pacing guide development can continue with a focus on instruction (Figure 2.6, p. 20). We suggest that teachers come together to share instructional activities and approaches that work well with the general population. These activities are described in the column named "General Instructional Activities." Working together with the teachers of students with special needs, the team also designs "Modified Instructional Activities" (the topic of Chapter 5). "Instructional Resources," which support the instruction of units are listed in the third column, might include any of the following: books, videotapes, software, web sites, guest speakers, field trips, and kits. Many of the activities appropriate for this extension of the pacing guide already may be specified in district curriculum guides or the teachers' manuals of textbooks.

Who Is Involved in the Process of Creating Pacing Guides?

We believe that the entire instructional staff of a school must be involved in the process of creating pacing guides. This includes the principal and other administrators, core subject teachers, specialty subject or elective teachers, and instructors who provide services to students with special needs such as teachers of special education, English as a Second Language (ESL), and the gifted. We also believe that district level personnel can and should be used as resources in the development process; they should *not direct* the process.

Figure 2.5. Pacing Guide (Assessment Component)

Subject/Grade Level _____ Year _____ Authors _____ Page# _____

Mid-Unit Assessments	End-of-Unit Assessments

Figure 2.6. Pacing Guide (Instructional Component)

Subject/Grade Level _____ Year _____ Authors _____ Page# _____

General Instructional Strategies	Modified Instructional Activities	Instructional Resources

Administrative Roles

The principal sets the tone for the task by emphasizing its importance and placing this work within the context of the overall school improvement process. The principal moves the work ahead by providing both pressure and support. Pressure comes in the form of deadlines, feedback, and a general expectation of accountability. Support is provided through technical assistance, clerical help, time, and other resources.

It is essential that the principal take the leadership role in the process. Instructional leadership can be exhibited by introducing the idea, participating in and monitoring the writing of the pacing guides, coordinating a production timetable, acquiring technical support such as district-level subject specialists, allocating clerical support so that teachers' time is not spent formatting and retyping documents, and reviewing and providing feedback on the pacing guides. Certain aspects of leadership may be delegated to grade-level chairpersons at the elementary level and department chairs in secondary schools, but we believe the principal must be the prime mover of this project. Guiding this process is instructional leadership at its best.

Core Teacher Roles

We believe that the concept of pacing guides loses much of its power if all teachers are not involved. Thus it is essential that all teachers who instruct a particular subject participate in developing the pacing guide. For example, at the elementary school level all third grade teachers who teach social studies would write the third grade social studies pacing guide. Consequently, at the elementary school level, most teachers should participate in the construction of several different pacing guides (typically four: language arts/reading, mathematics, social studies, and science) on their grade level, unless they are creating fewer interdisciplinary guides (see Figure 2.4). In the high school mathematics department a teacher may participate in the construction of two or three different course pacing guides (e.g., Algebra I, geometry, and math analysis) depending on the number of different course preparations assigned that year.

Core teachers should also review core pacing guides in contiguous grade levels, trying to achieve a smoothly articulated curriculum; core teachers should also read specialty or elective course pacing guides, searching for means of mutual support. In addition, they need to work together with teachers of students with special needs to coordinate efforts and to modify instruction to ensure the learning of essential curriculum objectives.

Specialty and Elective Teacher Roles

All courses need a pacing guide. To say that we only need pacing guides for core subjects is to belittle the significance of specialty and elective courses. In many cases, especially at the elementary school level, there may not be a detailed curriculum guide for a specialty course such as Fifth Grade Health and Physical Education or First Grade Music. The pacing guide, therefore takes on even greater significance, because once developed, it serves as the curriculum guide. At the elementary level it also is common for the specialist in art, music, technology, or physical education to be the only teacher in the building instructing in this discipline. Who forms the committee in this case? We suggest that it is beneficial to approach this problem in one of three ways; each approach has different benefits and problems. The art specialists from several schools can come together to produce grade-level art pacing guides. This strategy results in greater district-wide uniformity. A second approach is for the art, music, technology, and physical education specialists from one school to work together in planning their pacing guides. This coordinated approach results in greater integration of these subjects within the school. Finally, specialists may work with grade-level teams to design pacing guides that support core programs at each grade level. Although this strategy has many benefits, it is problematic for specialists to schedule meetings with all of the different grade levels.

Regardless of the approach employed for the creation of pacing guides, specialty and elective teachers must review core teachers' pacing guides in search of areas of overlap and possible integration. This task is especially important in states with high-stakes accountability testing programs. Wherever possible, specialty and elective teachers should provide needed reinforcement and practice for key tested concepts in the core academic areas. Occasionally, it also is possible, and perhaps more appropriate, for a noncore teacher actually to introduce a core objective in language arts/reading, mathematics, science, or social studies.

At the high school level the symbiotic interaction of teachers of different disciplines may be approached in a somewhat different manner. Many states' accountability systems require that students pass a series of end-of-course tests to graduate. An Algebra I examination is a barrier test in many states. Some schools have addressed this problem by doubling the time spent in algebra class to the equivalent of two periods per day for one year or to one period of Algebra I for two years. Although a need for more time may be the answer for some students, more of the same kind of instruction may not be the answer for others. Another, and perhaps more creative, approach is to construct a team-taught class that matches Algebra I with a vocational course. The two teachers work together to construct units and a pacing guide, which provide opportunities for the practical application of algebraic concepts in the vocational area.

Roles for Teachers of Students with Special Needs

The primary role of teachers of students with special needs in the development of pacing guides is to collaborate with general education teachers to modify instruction for the students they serve. Therefore they must be familiar with the pacing guides of all grade levels and/or courses their students take. Teachers of special education, compensatory education, and ESL must focus their instructional efforts on the most essential (usually tested) objectives gleaned from the pacing guides. Teachers of students who are gifted must develop means to enrich and/or compact curriculum. During the creation or revision of pacing guides, teachers of students with special needs should be assigned to the grade level or department with whom they work most closely. Strategies for modifying instruction for students with special needs are discussed in Chapter 5.

The Role of the Library Media Specialist

The library media specialist must become familiar with all pacing guides. In a large high school with 100 or more different courses, this charge may be divided among librarians (assuming there are more than one). The guides become the blueprint for ordering new materials; for developing resource packages that include video, print, and electronic sources to support the instruction of units; for identifying scheduling conflicts in the planned use of scarce materials; and for assisting the media specialist in designing supportive research lessons.

When and Where are Pacing Guides Developed?

Ideally, time during the summer is set aside to develop pacing guides, and teacher stipends are earmarked to support this effort. We realize that often the supports for curriculum development efforts and staff development are not ideal. State and federal (ESEA) funding is available to support teacher development directly related to the new standards and testing program. Consequently, we will discuss the development of pacing guides using three time frames: the summer workshop, faculty meetings during the school year, and a combination of summer and faculty meeting work. Although minor adjustments may be made to pacing guides during the academic year, they should be revised annually based on the results of summative assessment data. We have found that it is best to wait until just before the beginning of the new school year to complete these revisions. Testing data are available for review at this time, and additionally, any new teachers hired are now available to participate in the process. Novice teachers generally are inexperienced regarding the sequence and duration of instructional units. After participating in the process of developing or revising pacing guides, they will have a much clearer understanding of the curriculum they are to teach and leave the meeting with two or three pages of pacing guide "gold."

Summer Workshop Development

In a typical summer workshop geared toward the development of pacing guides, two to five days are devoted to the project. In a two-day framework it is entirely possible to accomplish at least drafts of all required pacing guides. Five days allows a thorough review process. Figure 2.7 illustrates a suggested timetable for a five-day elementary school pacing guide development summer workshop. Figure 2.8 (p. 26) suggests a timetable for a two-day summer workshop to develop pacing guides in a secondary school; review and revision are accomplished during faculty meetings once the school year begins. Obviously all times are approximate; our experience suggests, however, that the schedules provided are reasonable, if appropriate clerical and technical supports are provided. We now look in detail at the five-day elementary workshop illustrated in Figure 2.7. Because five days in summer for pacing guide development may not be available in all schools, the workshop can be easily translated into different time formats as shown in Appendix I; therefore, we suggest that all readers peruse the next section.

Day 1: Reintroduce the Process; Draft Pacing Guides in Mathematics, Science, and Grades K–2 Specialty Areas

On Day 1 the process of creating pacing guides is reintroduced to the faculty. The reasoning and logic that support the process are detailed; the timetable for draft completion, review, and revision is distributed. Obviously, this will not be the first time that faculty members have heard of "pacing guides." Prior to the summer workshop, the idea will have been discussed with the school improvement team/faculty advisory group. Support for using valuable time in this manner must be developed. Although the principal may lead the process, faculty must be in agreement that this is a worthwhile endeavor.

The faculty then divides into grade level and specialty area groups. The third grade works together; the fifth grade works together. Teachers of students with special needs are assigned to the grade levels with whom they work most closely. If a teacher of students with special needs works with two grade levels, it is appropriate to split time between them. It also might be wise to adjust the schedule to accommodate special needs teachers' areas of emphasis. For example, if a special education teacher works with both the second and the third grades in the areas of language arts/reading and mathematics, grade 2 pacing guides in language arts/reading and mathematics could be constructed on Day 1, and grade 3 guides in language arts/reading and mathematics could be designed on Day 2. Social studies and science guides would be written on the alternate days. With this scheduling flip, the special educator now is able to contribute to both grade levels in which the educator works.

Figure 2.7. Elementary Pacing Guide Timetable: Development, Review, and Revision During a Five-Day Summer Workshop

Time Frame		Core Teachers	Specialty and Elective Teachers	Special Needs Teachers
Day 1	3 Hours	Mathematics Guide	Kindergarten Specialty Guide Grade 1 Specialty Guide	Assigned to Core Team
	3 Hours	Science Guide	Grade 2 Specialty Guide	Assigned to Core Team
Day 2	3 Hours	Social Studies Guide	Grade 3 Specialty Guide Grade 4 Specialty Guide Grade 5 Specialty Guide	Assigned to Core Team
	3 Hours	Language Arts Guide		Assigned to Core Team
Day 3	3 Hours	Review Lower Grade Core Guides	Review K–1 Core Guides	Assigned to Core Team
	3 Hours	Review Higher Grade Core Guides	Review 2–3 Core Guides	Assigned to Core Team
Day 4	3 Hours	Review Specialty Area Guides	Review 4–5 Core Guides	Assigned to Core Team
	3 Hours	Revise Core Guides	Revise Specialty Guides	Assigned to Core Team
Day 5	6 Hours	Polish and Publish	Polish and Publish	Assigned to Core Team

Figure 2.8. Secondary Pacing Guide Timetable: Development during a Two-Day Summer Workshop with Review and Revision During Faculty Meetings after the School Year Begins

Time Frame		Core Teachers	Elective Teachers	Special Needs Teachers
Day 1	3 Hours	Core Course 1 Guide	Elective Course 1 Guide	Assigned to Core Team
	3 Hours	Core Course 2 Guide	Elective Course 2 Guide	Assigned to Core Team
Day 2	3 Hours	Core Course 3 Guide	Elective Course 3 Guide	Assigned to Core Team
	3 Hours	Core Course 4 Guide	Elective Course 4 Guide	Assigned to Core Team

Faculty Meetings after School Begins

Session 1	2 Hours	Review lower sequential core course guides.	Review lower sequential elective course guides.	Assigned to Core Team
Session 2	2 Hours	Review higher sequential core course guides.	Review higher sequential elective course guides.	Assigned to Core Team
Session 3	2 Hours	Review related elective course guides	Review related core and elective course guides	Assigned to Core Team
Session 4	2 Hours	Revise Core Course 1 & 2 Guides	Revise Elective Course 1 & 2 Guides	Assigned to Core Team
Session 5	2 Hours	Revise Core Course 3 & 4 Guides	Revise Elective Course 3 & 4 Guides	Assigned to Core Team

Core teachers work together with teachers of students with special needs to write pacing guides in mathematics and science on Day 1. We suggest beginning with mathematics because we believe the sequential nature of mathematics makes completion of this pacing guide the most straightforward and therefore a good place to begin. We follow with science because of the obvious interdisciplinary connections. Primary teachers may decide to take an interdisciplinary approach; regardless, two days are allocated for their pacing guides to be completed. If such an approach is taken, teachers must be careful to ensure that all objectives in all disciplines are instructed.

Specialty teachers most likely will work together as a group. On Day 1 they focus on creating draft pacing guides for grades K–2. As previously discussed it is typical to have only one person per specialty area in most elementary schools. If a structure for designing pacing guides across schools in these areas has not been designed, we suggest that they form a single committee. Each specialty teacher develops guides independently, but the committee serves as a sounding board for ideas. Specialty teachers also may discover areas of overlap that lead to an interdisciplinary approach.

After reintroducing the process, school administrators, including, if possible, central office supervisors and the superintendent, rotate among working groups offering support, encouragement, and ideas! If more than one school administrator is available, they may be assigned to participate in the work of specific groups.

Day 2: Draft Pacing Guides in Social Studies, Language Arts/Reading, and Grades 3–5 Specialty Areas

On Day 2 core teachers and teachers of students with special needs focus on social studies and language arts/reading. The experience of completing guides in mathematics, science, and social studies helps teachers with construction of the most difficult guide, language arts/reading. Specialty area teachers create guides for grades 3–5. Administrators continue to circulate and participate.

Day 3: Review Process

To ensure proper articulation among grade levels, a day is scheduled for core teachers and the teachers of students with special needs to review pacing guides both one grade level below and one grade level above their level. To facilitate this process draft guides must copied and distributed accordingly on the morning of Day 3. Written comments can be shared; if at all possible, face-to-face discussion should be structured to occur among teachers of consecutive grade levels.

Specialty teachers begin their review of core pacing guides on Day 3. K–1 pacing guides are reviewed in the morning; guides from grades 2 and 3 are reviewed in the afternoon. Specialty teachers identify areas of possible overlap and ways to support the instruction of core objectives.

School administrators work as a team to review and provide feedback to all working groups. Their efforts focus on articulation, continuity, and possible integration.

Day 4: Review and Revision

On the morning of Day 4, core teachers, working with the teachers of special needs students, review specialty area guides for their grade levels. Core teachers attempt to identify areas of mutual support. Would it make sense to teach a core unit at a different time because it blends well with a music unit? Perhaps the physical education teacher could have our first grade students count their jumping jacks by 2s, 5s, or 10s to support the instruction of this concept? Could the art teacher emphasize dress and costume during our unit on the social history of the colonies? If at all possible, the schedule is constructed so that face-to-face contact with all specialty teachers can be arranged for each grade level to facilitate this collaboration.

Also on the morning of Day 4, specialty area teachers complete their review of core pacing guides with grades 4 and 5. The afternoon is spent reflecting on the review information received from core teams and beginning the process of revising specialty guides for all grade levels.

Day 5: Revise, Polish, and Publish

Day 5 is spent completing all aspects of the process. Review information is considered, and final pacing guides in all areas are constructed. These guides are submitted to the school administration for final publication and distribution.

The five-day workshop just outlined is only one possibility for scheduling the completion of the pacing guides. In Appendix I, we provide several other possible timetables for this work. It may be more advantageous to spread some of the work into the school year when teachers are working with students. For example, the timetables detailed in Figure 2.8 (p. 26) and Appendix I (p. 103) suggest that the initial drafts of pacing guides be developed in a two-day summer workshop and that the review and revision of the guides be accomplished over several faculty meetings once the school year has begun.

How is the Process of Creating Pacing Guides Led and Managed?

Regardless of the schedule for the completion of the pacing guides, it is the responsibility of the principal to ensure that the process keeps moving. It is the principal who conveys the importance of this activity with his or her participation and support. What are the ways in which a principal can demonstrate this leadership?

Taking Charge of the Process

Someone must initiate, support, and monitor the process of creating pacing guides. Although this effort could be delegated to an assistant principal or teacher, we believe the importance of this work requires the leadership of the principal. The principal should be intimately involved in introducing the process, setting the timeline for completion, marshaling resources for support, providing feedback on draft efforts, and ensuring that the pacing guides actually become an integral part of instructional planning in the school. By providing this leadership and follow-through, the principal increases the likelihood that the process will be completed and implemented.

Finding the Time

Whenever we work with groups of teachers, we ask the following question: What is the most important support you need to complete this task successfully? The unanimous response is always a resounding "TIME!" We realize that the creation of pacing guides takes time. With everything that must be accomplished in schools, where can we find time to complete another important task?

Earlier we suggested the possibility of scheduling two- to five-day summer workshops; sample schedules for such sessions are included in Appendix I. If your district or school has the wherewithal to fund this workshop, we believe this is a good way to begin. Otherwise, time during or after the regular school day must be allocated for the project. Pacing guide work sessions can be conducted in place of faculty meetings. In elementary and middle schools, grade-level common planning time can be devoted occasionally to this work, although it is usually impossible to involve specialty teachers and special needs teachers together with the core team at this time. After-school departmental meeting time at the high school level also can be devoted to the development of pacing guides. Occasionally it also may be appropriate to use substitutes to free teachers for collaborative work. Finding time is undoubtedly the greatest challenge in this process. Perhaps the best way is to mix and match approaches. For example, we could start with a two-day workshop, followed by three faculty meetings, followed by three common planning times, followed by a full-day when a substitutes are provided for a grade level or department.

Training and Examples

If a principal or assistant principal is well versed in the process of creating pacing guides, it may not be necessary to seek outside assistance. It may, however, be useful to have an outside expert share his or her experiences in this process. It also is useful for teachers to view a variety of examples. The advantage of sharing examples is that teachers see that the work before them is not overwhelming; a pacing guide of two or three pages is not a difficult document to create. The disadvantage of sharing examples is that teachers may think that "this is the way to do it," and thereby creativity is blocked. We share a variety of examples using a variety of formats in Appendices III (p. 111), IV (p. 119), and V (p. 131); feel free, however, to invent your own.

Clerical Support

We can reduce the stress on teachers significantly by providing them with clerical support. We want our teachers to spend their time thinking about and discussing the best approaches to pacing and instruction, not worrying about the appearance of their documents. Thus, we suggest that paraprofessionals, secretarial staff, and/or parent volunteers be utilized to reformulate draft pacing guides into professional-looking documents. Of course, the professional format may differ depending on the audience. This may mean that a standardized chart format is created for teachers, a three-fold brochure is designed for parents, and/or a "pacing guide" website is developed to share with other schools and the community at large. Regardless, the professional appearance of the final documents should not be the responsibility of teachers; the professional content of the documents is their responsibility.

Materials

Another means for supporting this effort is to ensure that all necessary materials are available for work sessions. Consequently, blank forms, chart paper, markers, notebook computers, tape, and any other physical supplies should be readily available. In addition, any necessary content materials such as district curriculum guides, old pacing guides, the school calendar, and the testing blueprint should be provided. Again, we demonstrate the importance of this work and the value we place on teachers' time by supporting their efforts in as many ways as possible.

As a central office administrator, one of us compiled a CD-ROM for each elementary grade level, K–5. The CD contained a pacing guide template and electronic copies of curriculum guides for the four core subjects. By copying and pasting the objectives, essential skills, and content outlines from the curriculum to the pacing guide template, teachers saved hours of copying and typing. In the year prior to generating this resource, our instructional services office spent several weeks typing and formatting pacing guides for teachers. By anticipating and providing the most important resource materials needed to easily produce the pacing guide electronically, we saved both teachers and our office hours of work.

Data

Data regarding students' performance are important to review prior to creating or revising pacing guides. We advise that teachers be directly involved with formulating school improvement goals based on data interpretation. If student achievement data are organized in a manner that is easily understood, the interpretation of data becomes a straightforward task. Again, teachers should not spend their time crunching numbers or creating data displays; their time should be spent discussing, interpreting, and formulating improvement goals. Consequently, the principal must organize and present data to the working teams in a user-friendly format. We also advise that the principal complete his or her own evaluation of the available data; however, we believe that he or she should allow teachers to formulate their own hypotheses regarding the data, and that the principal's interpretation should be shared only to reinforce teachers' conclusions or to point out trends in the data that have been missed.

Feedback

Once draft pacing guides have been completed, they should be reviewed by a variety of groups: core teachers at other levels, specialty teachers, district support staff, and the school principal. Whereas reviewing the guides is time-consuming, it is important for the school principal to reinforce teachers' hard work, to learn as much as possible about all curriculum areas, and to offer suggestions where appropriate. If teachers turn in pacing guides and receive no feedback, they begin to suspect that this effort is just another superficial paper chase.

Follow-Through

Even more important than feedback on the draft guides is the need to provide follow-through. Once draft guides have been written, the principal must ensure that the review, publication, and distribution processes occur. Finally, through the use of "staffing meetings," the principal ensures that pacing guides actually do guide the delivery of curriculum. (This process will be explored in detail in Chapter 4.)

Permission to Fail

One concern of school-based administrators and central office personnel is the ability of teachers to create the best plan for pacing their courses. They wonder whether teachers have the requisite skills and knowledge to complete this task. Why not ask district subject supervisors, who are the real experts in the discipline, to create the best pacing guide? This approach would save lots of time for teachers. Simply give teachers the pacing guide and ask them to follow it. Although this approach would take less time and perhaps result in a more polished product, we believe that two major benefits of the project would be lost: the learning that occurs for teachers and the team bond that develops among colleagues. As teachers discuss, debate, and compromise, their understanding of the complexities of their curriculum increases; they become better teachers. When they collaborate with their peers in the creation of a plan that is superior to what any one of them could have developed individually, the team draws closer together.

If we simply hand teachers a pacing guide and say, "Follow this plan," a number of negatives will result: Teachers are less likely to follow the guide because they have no ownership in it; teachers miss a learning opportunity when they do not work together to design the guides; and teachers' accountability for students' learning is diluted because we have given them an excuse. If students perform poorly, a teacher can say, "But I followed *your* pacing guide!"

What happens if teachers create a faulty plan? We believe this is highly unlikely if the review and revision process is carried through. It is possible, however, that a pacing guide could be created that ignores a critical set of objectives and consequently results in poor student achievement. If this happens, we learn from our mistakes and revise for next year. In the long run, we believe that teacher ownership of the pacing guide and accountability for students' learning will pay off. We may occasionally fail, but if we continue to learn from our mistakes and improve, the long-term benefits will be great.

Perspective

This book, and this chapter in particular, focus on the development of pacing guides, one of many strategies for raising student achievement. Although the design and use of pacing guides is important, it is only one part of an overall school improvement process. And although the curriculum objectives we place on the guides are important, they are not the only topics we should teach our students. And although students' achievement on standardized tests is important, it is not the only way we measure their performance. A principal of a school must exercise leadership by placing the development of pacing guides into a broader context, nested within a school's systemic effort to improve students' achievement, the totality of teachers' work, and the depth and breadth of what we believe our students' education truly should be.

3

Creating Pacing Guides: The Assessment Component

In Chapter 2, we described a process for creating the curriculum component of pacing guides on which we sequence the content and skills to be taught, and we tied them to a proposed time schedule. In the next phase of pacing guide development, teachers plan for the assessment component of student learning. Once assessments have been administered, we recommend that teachers work together to interpret the results. In these discussions, which we have termed "staffing meetings" (see Chapter 4), teachers use assessment information to draw conclusions about what and how students are learning. Armed with these data, teachers revisit their pacing guides, adjusting and revising to respond to students' current needs.

Although we have described the planning process as a linear one (objectives first, then pacing, followed by assessment design and instructional planning), we acknowledge that effective planning doesn't always happen this way. There are many good reasons for changing the order of these steps. For example, it often makes sense for teachers to develop objectives and assessment methods first and then predict how much time will be required for most students to succeed at the expected level. Pacing, in this case, comes *after* assessment planning.

The reality is that most teachers don't think in linear steps at all. They might first consider objectives, then think about what activities fit those objectives best. In generating activity ideas, a team of teachers might develop a project that will later serve as a performance assessment. In thinking about what students will need to do to succeed on this assessment, the teachers may recognize a need to set a higher standard or notice that the assessment task forms a natural connection between two objectives they had planned to teach separately. This would then send them back to revise, add to, or change the sequence of the pacing guide goals.

Because the curriculum–instruction–assessment match is so critical, it is desirable for teachers to consider each of these components continually as they are planning. Good planning means constantly examining and reexamining objectives, assessment tools, and instructional strategies. The process is more like a web than a straight line.

In recommending the use of a pacing guide as a planning tool, it is our intention to describe a planning process that we believe is accessible and easily implemented, but that prompts teachers to tackle important curriculum and instructional issues. The pacing guide, then, serves as a clear and straightforward starting point for a complex process. As teachers move into conversations about the assessment and instruction components, the curriculum pacing guide must be on the table. It will be referred to, discussed, and modified, and it will become a record of teachers' best thinking as they plan.

In this chapter we will provide guidelines and ideas for teachers to consider as they plan for assessment of student learning. We will address the following questions:

- Why include assessment plans in a pacing guide?

- What are the sources of assessment information?

- How are assessments described in the pacing guide?

- Where in the pacing guide should assessments be included?

- What assessments should be included on the pacing guide?

- How can assessments be designed to provide meaningful information?

- How can teachers use assessment information?

Why Include Assessment Plans in a Pacing Guide?

A pacing guide is a road map for instruction. Like any other map, it serves as a guide to help teachers and students reach their destinations. Along the way, teachers should consult the map frequently to check their progress. Are we making good time? Should we take a short cut? A detour? Another route altogether? Perhaps we need to spend more time in one place and less in another? In the instructional context, answering these questions requires regular, frequent assessment of student learning.

Aligning Teaching and Learning

The curriculum component of the pacing guide is essentially a tool for aligning curriculum and instruction. When teachers consider all of the content and skills to be taught during the year and assign a time for each, they are matching what is written in the curriculum to what is actually going to be taught in the classroom. The assessment component of pacing guide development is also about alignment—the alignment of what is taught with what is learned.

Imagine a classroom in which teaching and learning are perfectly aligned. In this classroom, the teacher follows his curriculum pacing guide to the letter, and because students learn everything he teaches, he makes few revisions in his plan. A homecoming assembly, a snow day, and an unanticipated visit by the governor prompt minor adjustments, but still the teacher is able to predict with confidence what knowledge and skills his students will have at the end of the year. No students will struggle to make sense of concepts, fail to master skills, or display gaps in their understanding. Sometimes we may wish we taught in such a classroom, but the reality is that what is learned almost never equals what is taught. For that reason, we need assessment information. It is this information that reveals the discrepancies between what the teacher intended for students to learn and what they actually learned. When teachers have this information, they know the instructional needs of their students and can adjust their plans to meet those needs.

Data for Decision Making

When pacing guides and instructional plans do need revision, those revisions should be based on solid evidence of student needs. As teachers listen to and interact with their students, they are constantly noting difficulties students may be having understanding content or performing skills. On a day-to-day basis, teachers adjust instructional plans based on general observation of students at work, anecdotal evidence (like student questions), and even "gut feelings." We believe that all these sources of insight into student learning can be valuable, but we also know that frequent collection and review of actual assessment data from each student is necessary.

First, data from assessments help teachers check and confirm (or revise) their perceptions about what individual students are learning. A student who rarely participates in class discussion but always completes homework accurately may be perceived by the teacher to be progressing well, but in fact may be a struggling student who is getting regular assistance with homework. A student who fails to turn in assignments and is often absent from class may already know most of the course content, and may in fact be more successful with more challenging material.

Second, data from the students as a group are helpful feedback to teachers as they review and revise their pacing guides and lesson plans. Patterns in assessment results (such as a particular skill that is a weakness for many students, or a single test question missed by a large portion of the class) often cause teachers to reexamine their instructional strategies and reteach using a different approach.

A third benefit of careful and systematic assessment planning is the ability to use classroom tests (or other types of assessment tools) to predict student performance on large-scale, high-stakes tests. For assessments to be useful in this way, the pacing guide must include the content and skills to be tested in, for example, a state-mandated test. The classroom assessments must then be matched to the pacing guide. With this alignment in place, teachers can use their classroom assessments for early identification of student needs and can address these needs before students take the high-stakes test.

What are the Sources of Assessment Information?

Mandated State or District Tests

State testing of student learning is a long-standing practice in many states. Though the reauthorization of ESEA in 2002 made such testing mandatory for states to receive federal education funds, the kinds of tests used from state to state vary. Frequently, local school districts also implement their own testing programs. Districts may want more frequent testing of the state-mandated standards to track student progress from year to year. They may test regularly to identify student needs early, so that intervention can be provided before students take the state tests. School districts may also implement their own testing programs to measure student performance in areas that are not included in the state's testing program. Because all teachers want their students to meet or surpass the academic standards set by their districts and states, student success on these measures is an important goal.

State and district-wide tests are most commonly administered at the end of the school year, making their results of limited use to teachers as they monitor and adjust instruction for a group of students. However, student data from the spring of one school year is very useful to those teachers who will be teaching these students the *next* school year. Especially in cases where student data can be examined by skill area, teachers can use the students' spring results as they would any pretest data, to guide them in determining the academic strengths and needs of various individuals and groups. For example, suppose that a team of two sixth grade math teachers meets to review the fifth grade math results of their incoming students. Rather than looking at average scores for the group, or even individual students' overall scores, they examine the students' performance on several subtests within fifth grade math. In doing so, they discover that this group of students has scored significantly higher in problem solving and applications than in computation. This discovery leads the teachers to compare problem-solving and computation scores for individual students. Through this process, they are able to identify a significant number of students who need remediation in the areas of basic math facts and multiplication/division algorithms. Using the subtest data, the two teachers group these students together in one class for the coming year and adjust the pacing guide for that class to reflect a longer remediation and review period before moving into the sixth grade content.

Students do not participate in large-scale testing of every content area every year, and so teachers meeting to develop pacing guides do not always have this kind of student achievement data with which to begin. Even in the absence of specific student data, however, large-scale tests can be helpful. We encourage teachers to become as familiar as possible with the content and format of their state and district tests, and with the relative emphasis of various skills and topics on the tests. Information about what the test looks like, what skills and content receive the most emphasis, and what test-taking strategies students need is essential to planning the assessment component of the pacing guide.

It is our hope that teachers will not come to view their classes as nothing more than training grounds for state tests. To do so would be to deny students access to the most meaningful purposes of education and motivations to learn. At the same time, it would also be unfair to deprive students of the preparation they need to succeed on large-scale tests, the results of which may determine the opportunities open to them in the future.

Our view is that students succeed best when they learn in highly interactive and student-centered classrooms, where learning targets are clear, activities are engaging, and relationships among learners are important. We believe that it is not only possible but imperative that students be prepared to demonstrate their skills and understandings in the classroom context, as well as on the high-stakes, standardized tests they will encounter.

Classroom Assessments

Despite their importance, large-scale tests do not provide teachers with sufficient information to guide instruction. These tests are designed primarily for accountability purposes, rather than to inform instruction. They are administered too infrequently to serve as guideposts for instructional decision making, and their formats do not always reflect how students learn. In addition, the information that schools receive about student performance on large-scale tests sometimes consists of a set of scores alone, which is of limited use in guiding instructional decisions.

Assessments that teachers design (or select) and build into their instruction supplement state testing programs with more frequent, targeted, and context-ualized measures of student learning. As all teachers know, students come to the classroom with a range of experiences and prior knowledge. Some need more review and reinforcement than others. They have a variety of learning styles and respond in many ways to any single lesson. Some are more interested than others in any particular unit of study. Good assessment information is es-sential to gain insight in to *how much* students understand and *how well* they un-derstand it. Later in this chapter, we will provide guidelines and recommenda-tions for classroom assessment design.

Putting It All Together

We cannot overemphasize the importance of using a range of tools to assess student learning. We believe that to get a complete picture of student perfor-mance, teachers need information from large-scale tests as well as a variety of types of classroom assessments. Taken together, information from this range of assessment tools will help teachers answer questions like:

- ♦ How are students (both individuals and groups) doing in relation to the goals identified in our pacing guides?

- ♦ If they *are not* meeting the goals we set, what are their current needs?

- ♦ If they *are* meeting the goals we set, could they be learning more than we originally predicted?

- ♦ In what ways (and for whom) do we need to adjust instruction to maximize learning for every student?

How are Assessments Described on the Pacing Guide?

Providing Specific Assessment Information

When we work with teachers to develop pacing guides, we encourage them to describe their assessments rather specifically or to simply attach a copy of the assessment itself to the guide. At first, this may appear to be excessive paper-work—after all, teachers know what their assessments look like, so why should they describe them on this document? As we did with the curriculum compo-nent, we will encourage teachers to use the assessment component of their pac-ing guides to check their own curriculum-instruction-assessment alignment. If the information on the assessment component of the pacing guide is relatively specific, it can be shared much more easily.

To illustrate, suppose that a teacher's pacing guide simply notes "test" at the end of an instructional unit. This could mean a number of things. For example:

- ♦ "Test" could mean that a teacher plans to administer an end-of-chapter test taken directly from a textbook. If so, the match between what this test measures and the goals on the pacing guide must be examined. It may be that not all the test items are directly related to the learning goals, or that the test does not give the same degree of emphasis to certain topics as the pacing guide does.

- ♦ "Test" could mean that the teacher has developed a test that is closely related to the content and skills described on the pacing guide, but plans to average this grade with class participation, homework, and other grades. Is this a fair assessment of students' performance on the goals?

- ♦ "Test" could mean that students will be working together in cooperative groups to complete an end-of-unit project, which they will then present to the class. If this is the scenario, then teachers must discuss how they will document what each individual student has learned.

To make the description of an assessment specific enough to be useful in checking alignment and planning, we suggest that the pacing guide include what learning is being assessed, the type of assessment tool being used, and (where appropriate) how it will be administered and scored.

Where in the Pacing Guide Should Assessments Be Included?

The pacing guide format in Chapter 2 provides space to record decisions and ideas about plans for assessing essential skills, end-of-unit goals, and mid-unit skills and understandings. Teachers can complete these sections of the pacing guide in a number of ways; our suggestions and guidelines are presented in the next section. The two examples that follow (Figures 3.1 and 3.2) illustrate how the assessment component of a pacing guide might look.

Figure 3.1. Excerpt from the Assessment Portion of a Pacing Guide

Subject/Grade Level _____   Social Studies Grade 4   Year_____
Authors _____   Page# 1

Mid-Unit Assessments	*End-of-Unit Assessments*
(Map skills) 1. Quiz on map components 2. "Complete-the- map activity." Partners use rubric to check for essential elements. 3. "Plan a trip" project. Students work in groups, present projects; classmates use rubrics to provide feedback.	Each student is given a map of a state, the names of two destinations within that state, and a starting point within that state. Using the "Plan-a-trip" rubric and their group projects as models, create an itinerary and driving directions for the trip (to be scored by teacher using the rubric).

What Assessments Should Be Included in the Pacing Guide?

We have mentioned that most teachers are *always* assessing student learning. From their conversations, observations, and daily interactions with students, teachers gain information about what students know and can do, as well as what help they need. Teachers who are experts at informal, ongoing assessment know how to embed it so completely into instruction that students are continuing to learn at the same time the teacher is collecting assessment information. This daily assessment produces highly valuable information and feedback for teachers and enables them to address student needs as they are teaching. At the same time, it is not the purpose of the pacing guide to serve as a record of ongoing, daily assessment. Rather, the assessments noted on the pacing guide are more formal "checkpoints" of student learning and are generally administered to the entire class.

Figure 3.2. Excerpt from the Assessment Portion of a Pacing Guide, U.S. Government

Subject/Grade Level_____ Social Studies Grade 11 Year_____
Authors_____ Page# 1

Mid-Unit Assessments	*End-of-Unit Assessments*
(Writing skills) 1. Pre-writing outline of candidates' positions. 2. Graded essay response to class debate. 3. Graded "editorial"—persuasive techniques applied. (Summarize, interpret, and provide strong rationale for views and positions on political issues) 1. "Editorial" project: Students work in groups, present editorials from various newspapers, and interpret them from selected points of view. 2. Outline of candidates' positions.	Writing task: Based on the candidates' positions on the five major election issues we've discussed, determine which candidate you would support. Assume that you were hired by your candidate's campaign to write a speech that will be delivered by the candidate at our school. You were selected because you strongly support this candidate; and because you know the population of the school well enough to understand which issues interest our students and which arguments they will find persuasive. Write the speech.

It goes without saying that formal assessment planning begins by examining the learning objectives listed in the curriculum component of the pacing guide. This is where teachers have carefully delineated what they want students to know and be able to do, and it is from these objectives that assessments are drawn. Although this relationship between objectives and assessment appears obvious, our experience suggests that a close match is not always so easy to achieve. We recommend that the pacing guide indicate the nature of assessments of *essential skills, unit goals,* and *mid-unit checkpoints.*

Assessment of Essential Skills

Ironically, the most difficult objectives to assess are often the most important things for students to learn. Though it can be a difficult task (every teacher wants students to learn more than just two or three things), we encourage teachers to consider the question, "What are the *essential skills* you're teaching—the bottom-line things you wouldn't want students to leave your class without learning?" Each discipline has fundamental content and skills that students carry with them and use in their lives beyond school. For example, English teachers generally say that being a good writer is more important than diagraming a sentence. Understanding sentence structure is certainly a *component* of good writing, and sentence diagraming is a tool for understanding sentence structure. Still, neither the skill of diagraming nor knowledge of sentence structure is the real point. These are simply steps along the road to developing skill as a writer—the ability to write effectively is the real goal.

Because essential skills are generally broad, complex, and developed over a period of time, they can be difficult to assess. Teachers may find that to do a good job of assessing essential skills, they need to use tools such as performance assessment tasks, portfolios, or other formats that allow students to demonstrate the application of complex skills. We will discuss assessment formats further in later sections of this chapter.

Assessment of Unit Goals

After establishing the essential skills and content, we ask teachers to think about unit-level goals and assessments. As units of study are taught, students gain skills and knowledge that are component parts of the essential skills they're building. End-of-unit assessments serve as final or summative measures of student learning during the unit as well as tools for monitoring the continuing development of essential skills. For example, a series of science units might focus on simple machines, insects, geology, and plant reproduction. Within the context of each of these units, students are practicing process skills (the "essentials") such as isolating a variable, gathering and recording data, and supporting conclusions with evidence. Each unit will likely have its own assessment, which will document *both* the students' depth of understanding of the content *and* their continuing development of the essential skills.

Mid-Unit Checkpoints

Between the ongoing daily assessment that we've discussed and the administration of an end-of-unit assessment, most teachers see a need for mid-unit checkpoints of student learning. These occur in forms such as quizzes, short group projects, essays, notebook checks, and journals. Mid-unit assessments are particularly important when students are learning skills and concepts that are needed for further instruction. These are times when teachers know they need to verify that student are learning the component skills and concepts they need before going further with the unit.

For example, consider a goal like "Students will solve linear equations." During this unit, one would expect that students would discuss, solve, and graph many equations. They will probably learn more than one method for solving equations and will solve equations at increasing levels of difficulty. An end-of-unit assessment will be administered, but each of the steps along the way should also be assessed as students move toward competence in this very complex goal.

We suggest that mid-unit assessments, especially those that provide information about students' readiness to move on, be noted in the assessment component of the pacing guide.

How Can Classroom Assessments Be Designed to Provide Meaningful Information?

Begin with Clear Criteria

Setting criteria for student learning and performance is the first and most important step in assessment development. When teachers define criteria, they translate the goals from the pacing guide into language that clarifies what the goal will "look like" when students perform it. Criteria provide an explicit description of how students will demonstrate their learning. When learning goals are broad or complex, as is the case with many essential skills, clear criteria are especially important. An assessment based on solid criteria is likely to render meaningful information about what students really know and can do.

Consider the following criteria that describe student performance of *observation skills* in science:

♦ Observe carefully enough to notice detail that might not be immediately obvious to the casual observer.

♦ Observe using all appropriate senses, noticing sound, texture, and the like, as well as what can be seen.

♦ Use measurement and/or magnification tools to increase the accuracy of observations.

♦ Record observations for later reference and use.

These criteria allow both student and teacher to focus their attention on clear behaviors that describe "what good observers do." Whether the teacher is informally assessing students in the course of their daily activity or rating their observation skills and assigning a grade; we know there is a clear and shared definition of observing.

Choose the Right Assessment Tool

Once criteria have been established and shared with students, teachers can select from a range of tools for assessing student learning. To get the most complete picture possible of what students are learning, teachers are advised to use a variety of assessment types in the course of the school year. Each of the assessment tools shown below has its own purposes, advantages, and drawbacks. It is important for teachers to choose tools that are consistent with their instructional practice, that are valid measures of the learning being assessed, and that are understood by students. When choosing assessment tools, teachers might consider:

◆ *Controlled-response tests,* such as multiple choice, true/false, matching, or fill in the blank.

◆ *Essays,* in which students must extend, apply, or analyze the content they've learned.

◆ *Performance tasks,* such as demonstrations, projects, diagrams, and models.

◆ *Portfolios,* which engage students in the process of examining and critiquing their own work.

Teachers who are thoughtful about assessment understand that all of the assessment tools mentioned here have a place in most classrooms. Assessment techniques are not "good" or "bad" by virtue of their format. We've heard teachers proudly declare, "I've given up testing for good. Now I assess only with performance tasks!" Others say, "I've rewritten all my tests in multiple-choice format, so the students can practice for the state standardized test in the spring." We believe that most teachers need a *range* of assessment techniques because they are measuring a range of learning objectives. Techniques should be chosen and tools designed based on the content and skills being assessed.

The following checklists are intended only as suggestions and "starters" for teacher decision making. In reality there are no right or wrong answers to the question of which kind of assessment is best in any given situation. The quality of student assessment depends on how well the assessment tool is designed, how closely it matches the teacher's instructional approaches, what previous experience students have had, and a variety of other factors. However, we believe these guidelines are generally helpful in choosing an assessment tool.

◆ *A controlled-response test, such as multiple-choice, true/false, matching, or short answer should be considered when:*

• The emphasis is on students' retrieval of information.

• Skills, if tested with these formats at all, are discrete and not complex.

• The test is a mid-unit checkpoint.

- A sample of student learning, rather than a holistic picture, is sufficient.

- Instructional activities have been primarily teacher directed versus student centered.

♦ *An essay test is appropriate when:*

- The emphasis is on content, but a deep understanding that goes beyond recall is required.

- The teacher wants to provide an open-ended opportunity for students to construct a creative or highly analytical response.

- The test will require students to use their content knowledge by applying it in a new situation or to a new problem.

♦ *A performance assessment, such as a project, demonstration, or task is a good choice when:*

- Students can directly perform a skill or set of skills.

- Students can demonstrate their understanding in authentic, real-world contexts.

- Students can apply what they know and can do to a new problem or in a new situation.

- Classroom activities have been performance oriented and students have learned and practiced the skills required to do the task successfully.

♦ *A portfolio might be considered to:*

- Show examples of student performance of essential skills.

- Assess student learning in a holistic way—across an entire unit, course, or year of instruction.

- Document students' best work in a content area *or* show the progress they've made from the beginning to the end of the school year.

Plan Classroom Instruction that Supports Success on the Assessment

With clear criteria in mind and an assessment format selected, teachers should again check the alignment of assessment with instruction. Though it may seem overly obvious to point out that an assessment must measure the learning that's been taught, we know that experienced and highly skilled teachers check the instruction—assessment match regularly. Often, they select or design the end-of-unit test before instruction begins and make sure each lesson directly targets the skills and content to be tested. Depending on the format of the assessment, it can be desirable to share it with students at the beginning of the unit, so that they have a clear picture of what they will be expected to know and be able to do as a result of the unit.

Effective instruction not only helps students develop the skills and learn the content to be assessed; it also prepares them to deal successfully with the demands of the selected assessment format. Many teachers work hard to develop classroom assessments whose format mirrors that of the high stakes tests the students will take. Instruction, then, includes not only teaching the content and skills to be assessed, but also helping students understand how to navigate the testing format. We believe that this kind of test preparation is not only acceptable, but also important, and we do not consider it to be "teaching to the test" (a phrase that has come to connote negative practices that stop just short of cheating). On the contrary, students who know the content and can demonstrate the skills to be assessed should never be hampered by a testing format that is unfamiliar and confusing to them.

As teachers discuss their assessment design, the practice of making classroom assessments look like the state's large-scale tests begs the question, "How much of this is enough?" We continue to believe that students need opportunities to demonstrate their learning in a variety of ways, and so they need access to a range of assessment formats. We encourage teachers to ensure that their students are familiar enough with each assessment format so that it does not stand in the way of their performance. Beyond that, we question the value of continuing to "practice" a single format as a way of preparing for a high-stakes test.

Work in Collaborative Groups to Design Common Assessment Tools

Daily and *mid-unit assessments* are generally designed, administered, and interpreted by classroom teachers. Although we encourage teachers to share ideas and assessment tools with each other, we recognize that ongoing classroom assessment practices vary widely among teachers. Just as two teachers might use different instructional strategies to teach the same skill, so might those teachers collect informal assessment information in different ways.

End-of-unit assessments, however, have the potential to provide data that can inform planning across a grade level, department, or even a whole school. When teachers from several different classrooms who are teaching the same content can combine, compare, and examine assessment data, they are better equipped to collaborate in planning and decision making about instruction.

Therefore, we encourage teachers who are teaching the same units to design and use common assessments whenever it is practical to do so. The degree to which common assessments can be designed depends largely on the nature of the pacing guide. Teachers who work together from the beginning of the school year on a common pacing guide open the door to the design of common assessment instruments.

Many schools differentiate instruction by providing courses at different levels, such as standard, advanced, and honors versions of the same course. We recommend that the teachers of these classes collaborate both in the development of pacing guides and in the design and selection of assessments. Although their classes will likely move at different rates and study units in differing degrees of depth, these differences should not be random nor determined simply by the preferences of individual teachers. These teachers undoubtedly have a common core of instruction to plan and assess. We recommend building that common core together and then differentiating the levels in planned, purposeful ways.

Although it is outside the control of classroom teachers, the timing of state tests has a great influence on pacing guide development, as teachers generally use state testing dates as a framework into which their instruction and assessment must fit. Large-scale testing programs create the need for students to learn a predetermined set of content and skills by a particular date, yet the reality is that students learn at very different rates and in very different ways. The idea that everyone must be ready for the same test at the same time competes with the idea that good instruction is tailored to students' varying needs and rates of learning. This poses a challenge for teachers who are developing pacing guides. They must assess student learning often, use assessment information to identify students needing extra help or support, and find ways to offer that support while meeting their commitment to teach the content and skills that will be tested. This balancing act is yet another reason we encourage teachers to work in collaborative teams. When teachers of the same grade or course work together, their opportunities for flexible grouping, providing extra practice or reteaching, and other interventions are increased.

In Chapter 4, we will describe *staffing meetings* as opportunities for teachers to analyze data, discuss student needs and progress, and plan instruction together. Student assessment results from end-of-unit tests and projects can be valuable in these discussions. When teachers who are teaching the same content and skills use the same or similar assessment instruments, they have the information they need to make decisions about regrouping students for remediation or acceleration. They might also look for patterns in the data that indicate particular parts of the unit that were more difficult for students as a group and work together to design instruction that will address this need. Although individual teachers are sometimes reluctant to compare their own students' assessment data to those of other classes, a truly collaborative group of teachers might go so far as to examine the various methods and strategies they each used and discuss which appeared to be the most effective for particular groups of students.

How Can Teachers Use Assessment Information?

When assessment is carefully planned, valid, and meaningful, it yields valuable information about student learning. Although we tend to think about the assignment of a grade as the endpoint of the assessment process, a closer look reveals a variety of ways in which assessment information can be useful to teachers.

Monitoring and Adjusting Instruction During the School Year

With their pacing guides as frameworks, teachers use assessment information to monitor and adjust instruction. Sometimes, an individual student's assessment will show a need for reteaching or remediation. A student who consistently exceeds expectations may also need intervention in the form of enrichment or acceleration. In many cases, these needs can be met by modifying instruction within the classroom (a number of strategies for modifying instruction are described in Chapter 5). In other cases, teams of teachers may want to discuss moving students from group to group or creating small groups of students with similar needs. Staffing meetings, described in Chapter 4, are designed to provide a forum for this discussion.

Individual teachers may find that patterns and trends in the assessment results for a particular class show a need to adjust instruction for the whole group. For example, suppose a teacher is following the pacing guide he developed with his team. After a short time, classroom assessments show that many students simply aren't understanding the content and developing the skills well enough for him to move ahead with the next unit. One approach to this dilemma is to shrug, bemoan the students' lack of ability and motivation, and move ahead with the schedule. This teacher, faced with valuable assessment information that reveals students' needs, would be choosing to ignore both the data and the needs of students. This may be more convenient for the teacher, but it is certainly not in the best interest of students. A more responsible approach would be to acknowledge that these students need more instruction, and perhaps different instruction, to accomplish the goals. This is a time to revisit the pacing guide and determine what changes can be made to carve out the time needed for further instruction.

Reviewing and Assessing Pacing at the End of the Year

Near the end of the school year or early in the summer, an end-of-year review is conducted. The discussion here is similar to that at previous meetings but focuses on looking at a summary of all the available data and at the pacing guide as a whole. This includes the results not only of classroom assessments, but of the state tests as well. Teachers review the year in its entirety, comparing their plan (the pacing guide) to the results (the achievement data). They use this comparison to infer ways the pacing guide might be adjusted to maximize learning the following year. Over time, as teachers refine their pacing guides, they will become more and more comfortable with the sequence and timing of units. Then, the year-end review can become a forum for discussing what happens within each unit; that is, teachers can begin to research and share instructional and assessment strategies that help them implement the pacing guide in the most effective ways.

In some schools we have worked with, we have found that as pacing guide development is implemented schoolwide, student performance has improved over time. In these schools, the end-of-year review has become a time to discuss increasing expectations based on improved student performance in the preceding grades.

Providing Feedback to Students and Parents

Another way teachers use assessment information is to inform students and parents regarding the progress being made toward learning goals. Teachers use a range of vehicles for communicating this information. There are periodic formal reporting tools, such as report cards, narratives, and conferences (parent/teacher or student/parent/teacher). Many teachers also use informal methods to provide feedback, such as writing comments on student work and sending it home to be signed, or writing letters and notes to parents.

Regardless of the means by which assessment information is communicated, it is critical that parents understand not only *how* their children are doing in class, but also *what* they are learning. Although most parents are happy to see an A or a B on a report card, a grade alone gives them no substantive information about what their child is learning. We believe that parents can support learning better if they have a clear understanding of the goals and criteria the assessment is designed to measure. Just as we have encouraged teachers to share goals and criteria with students at the beginning of the instructional process, we also believe that parents should know what skills and content have been identified as essential to learn. When a grade is accompanied by supporting information that describes what the learning targets are and where the child's work is in relation to the targets, then assessment information can become descriptive and powerful.

Creating a Schoolwide Focus on Learning

When teachers work together to create pacing guides and clarify learning goals, exciting opportunities emerge for a schoolwide conversation about what and how students are learning. This discussion can be a natural extension of staffing meetings. The principal or leadership team can simply identify issues, concerns, or ideas that emerge from staffing discussions, and bring them to larger teams or to the faculty as a whole.

For example, consider a high school in which the math department operates independently from the social studies department, even though they serve the same students. These students may be studying statistics in math and then going down the hall to social studies to learn about polling data the next class period. If teachers don't help students make the important connections between mathematics and its applications in the world, students are unlikely to make these connections on their own.

We are familiar with an elementary school in which every teacher teaches reading, but where, until recently, second grade teachers had little information about their students' first grade reading experiences. Fourth grade teachers weren't sure what kind of reading assessment was used in third grade, and fifth grade teachers used a program they had learned about at a recent conference, which nobody else in the school had ever seen! In short, each grade level had its own reading program.

By working in cross-grade and cross-department groups, teachers can begin to set criteria that define learning goals that transcend individual units, subject areas, and grade levels. At the elementary level, this conversation might start with a question like, "What are the essential skills in reading at each grade level?" These skills, taken together, should form a clear sequence of criteria that define good reading. But do they? Are there gaps, or perhaps places where the continuum of skills is redundant? When one looks at the reading program from the point of view of a student who enters school at age five and stays for six years, does it seem coherent and well articulated?

At the secondary level, teachers can work together to generate criteria for skills that cut across various courses. For example, social studies and English teachers might collaborate on a set of criteria for a quality research paper, or the whole science department could agree on components of a quality lab report.

Predicting Student Performance on Future Assessments

Results from school-based assessments are valuable in predicting student performance on future assessments. For example, by using a sequenced series of math assessments and correlating their results over time with math results from standardized tests, teachers can often predict the performance of third or fourth graders on the math portion of the state test they will take as fifth graders. This predictive quality of assessment data is important because it allows teachers to diagnose needs and provide intervention to students *before* they take the large-scale test. This strategy can keep many students from falling behind, thereby increasing *both* their success as learners *and* their standardized test scores. Most teachers would agree that intervention is most effective when it is provided as early as possible, and that it is preferable to remediation *after* students have failed the test. Using school assessments as predictors of later achievement on large-scale tests can give faculties the information they need to move from remediation to intervention, helping to prevent failure rather than correct it.

Tracking the Progress of Students over Time

Data that describe the progress students make over a period of time complete the picture of how well students are learning. Schools generally have the data they need to describe what a student has learned between September and May of any given year. Often, they do not have assessments that track student progress on essential skills like reading, problem solving, or writing across more than one year. In cases where assessment tools are inconsistent or criteria are not established, a student can be rated as "above grade level" in May and in need of remediation by October! A series of assessments on the most essential, long-range learning goals can create a longitudinal profile that records the progress of individual or groups or children over time. Figure 3.3 (p. 52) shows a student's literacy development beginning in kindergarten and extending through fourth grade.

This literacy profile is particularly useful because teachers in the school have worked together to define what skills and behaviors characterize reading, writing, and spelling at the beginning, middle, and end of each grade level. Their assessments are commonly agreed-upon instruments, which are aligned with their expectations and are consistent from grade to grade. When a fourth grade teacher sees "mid-second grade" on a student's profile, he knows what criteria it represents.

Note that the student whose profile is shown in Figure 3.3 received additional help through various intervention programs beginning in the middle of

Figure 3.3. Literacy Development Profile

Grade Level (All results are SPRING end-of-grade data)	Reading	Writing	Spelling
K	End of K level	Mid-K level	End of K level
1	Mid-1 level	Mid-1 level	End of 1 level
2 Tutoring program began in February when assessment showed "early second grade." Also attended summer tutoring program.	End of 1 level	Early 2 level	Mid-2 level
3 Attended after-school literacy program 2× week.	Mid-3 level	End of 3 level	End of 3 level
4	Early 4 level	Mid-4 level	End of 4 level

second grade. By this time, it was clear that the student was falling behind. Even though second grade is not a year when students take *state tests* in this district, the school had the information it needed to get this student back on track. By the time the state test was given at the end of third grade, the student had already received intervention to help him bring his reading skills up to grade level.

When information like this is shared with parents annually or semi-annually, they can get a clear picture of their child's journey through school and compare their own child's performance to the standards and criteria that define expected performance at each grade level. It is important to explain to parents that children's learning very seldom proceeds at a constant rate. It is more common for children to have periods of rapid growth and other periods of slower growth. To expect exactly one year's worth of progress in each school year in an area like reading or writing is unrealistic. However, if teachers collect and examine data that describe student progress over time, then they can work with parents to determine when and in what areas children need extra help.

Longitudinal data is equally important when assessing the progress of high-achieving students. These students may come to school as kindergartners already reading, and their assessment results may show that they are well above grade level every year. Yet teachers still should have concerns about these students if they do not see significant growth. In Chapter 5 we discuss ways that teachers can modify instruction for a variety of learners in the classroom. Highly capable students are just as deserving of intervention as those who are struggling. We must be alert to the possibility that students who are very successful on our assessments may not be continuing to grow academically at the rates they should.

Informing the School Improvement Process

Once longitudinal data are collected, they can be important tools to inform the school improvement process. By combining the data to look at students in groups, teachers and principals can access valuable information about strengths and needs in their instructional programs.

School reform and program improvement are too often implemented one year at a time. One set of test scores is reviewed, and based on these data, annual goals are set. Programs and initiatives are quickly up and running, and by the end of the school year are evaluated. The next year, there's a new goal and the process starts all over again. Data that follow student progress over time can keep faculties and school communities focused on steady progress toward more long-range, challenging goals and can indicate whether or not various initiatives have any lasting effect on student learning.

Providing Accountability Information that Goes Beyond Standardized Tests

Assessment information that describes student learning across years or subject areas is very useful for accountability purposes. Many teachers and principals become frustrated when their schools are portrayed in the community and in the press as nothing more than one set of annual scores on the state-mandated standardized test, but schools are often unequipped to provide any other clear, meaningful data. Supplementing scores on state tests with school-based measures of student performance provides a more comprehensive view of what students know and can do and helps to put the large-scale test scores in a context.

Whether assessment planning becomes a schoolwide collaborative process or is simply implemented within teacher teams, it is a necessary component of instructional planning and of developing pacing guides. The best, most careful planning by teachers is an exercise in futility, unless it includes a mechanism for accessing and sharing meaningful information about what and how students are learning. We encourage teachers to include assessment planning in their pacing guide development and to rely on assessment results in their daily and long-range decision making.

4

Using Staffing Meetings to Monitor and Adjust Instruction

The creation of pacing guides and the collection of formative assessment data are necessary, but not sufficient, in our schoolwide process of planning and monitoring instruction. Both of these tasks involve considerable time and effort, and without an institutionalized structure for follow-up, they may become (especially in the eyes of overworked teachers) nothing more than another needless administrative attempt at micromanagement. Pacing guides need to be living documents, used weekly for lesson planning and in a constant state of revision. The use of formative assessment techniques and the systematic collection and analysis of the resultant data demand that we consider instructional changes.

Recent federal mandates requiring schools to disaggregate achievement data by subgroups of students (disability, minority, second language learners, etc.) make it especially important to monitor the progress of groups and individual students. It no longer is sufficient to show that the group as a whole is demonstrating achievement above benchmark criteria; we also must document that each subgroup of learners is making adequate progress toward these goals.

The tasks of pacing instruction, measuring students' progress, and planning instructional interventions have long been the responsibility of each individual teacher. Without burning out, lone teachers cannot adequately plan instruction, create, and administer multiple formative assessments; collect and analyze these data; and develop and implement instructional interventions in a manner that will result in the responsive academic classroom we desire. We believe that *mastery learning*, although theoretically appealing, was not successful because individual teachers were expected to provide reteaching, reassessment, and enrichment in their own classrooms without much support. All of these tasks are accomplished best within the supportive arms of a committed learning community. When teachers plan together, whether in the generation of pacing guides

55

(as described in Chapter 2), in the creation of formative assessments (as described in Chapter 3), or during the periodic review of students' progress (as described in this chapter), the collective wisdom of the professional team has a synergistic effect.

We recommend that staffing meetings be implemented schoolwide to provide a structure within which collaborative planning for student achievement can occur. In this chapter, we will discuss why staffing meetings are an important part of our process and how they can be organized and conducted most effectively.

Why are Staffing Meetings Important?

Put simply, we recommend that "staffing"[1] meetings be held in order to institutionalize what we know to be good practice. Given the many demands placed on teachers, the changing needs of students, and the occasional crisis, it's not hard to see why teachers rarely sit down together to reflect on the year-long plan for instruction and think about how well that plan is meeting the needs of students. Staffing meetings create a time, a place, and a plan for this important discussion to occur. We suggest that staffing meetings be held four (or more) times a year for the following purposes:

- ♦ To ascertain progress on the instructional calendar described on the pacing guide
- ♦ To revise pacing guides, if necessary
- ♦ To review formative assessment data
- ♦ To identify problem learning areas for the group as a whole, for small groups, or for individual students
- ♦ To select appropriate curriculum approaches and plan instructional interventions

The staffing meeting is roughly analogous to the child study meeting used as part of the special education referral process, except that the unit of analysis is a group of students, rather than an individual child.

---

1 We borrow the term *staffing* from our colleagues in psychology. Occasionally, when a student has needs beyond the means and knowledge of school personnel, we have assistance from colleagues at the local university. A team of professionals from a variety of disciplines is assembled to evaluate the child and suggest the best course of action. This meeting is called a *staffing*.

How are Staffing Meetings Organized?

To be effective, staffing meetings must be structured in a professional manner appropriate to the importance of the meeting. Staffing meetings are planned well in advance; all participants are informed regarding the schedule and their roles; applicable materials and data are available; an agenda is produced; minutes are recorded and distributed; and procedures for follow-up are employed.

Planning

We believe that it is the responsibility of the school principal to develop and establish the procedures for conducting staffing meetings. *To delegate this critical task is to abdicate the role of educational leader of the school.* The principal creates the yearly meeting schedule, determines the participants, ensures that relevant materials and data are available, assists in producing the agenda, arranges for minutes to be taken and distributed, and ensures that actions decided upon are followed through. The principal may chair the actual meetings or assign this role to teacher leaders, such as team leaders at the elementary and middle school levels or department chairs at the high school level. This places the locus of control closer to the classroom and also offers a unique opportunity to develop teacher leaders. In any case the principal must attend and be an active participant. The school administrator also facilitates the meeting by seeing to all organizational and clerical matters prior to and following the staffing.

Participants

The unit of analysis in the staffing meeting is the group of students engaged in a specific core subject(s). Thus, in elementary and middle schools, staffing meetings are conducted by grade level or by team. In high school, staffing meetings are conducted within departments. Specialty, elective, and/or exploratory teachers and teachers of students with special needs participate in all staffing meetings in which the students with whom they work are discussed. Therefore, the general music teacher and physical education instructor at the elementary school level may participate in six different staffing meetings, one each for kindergarten through grade five. Teachers of students with special needs who work with different grade levels also attend several meetings. Guidance counselors and media specialists often attend all staffings, as well. While the value of these meetings will be readily apparent to the participants, and the specialty and special needs teachers will be pleased that their core-teacher peers actually need and value their input, this is a burdensome number of meetings. Fairness dictates that these teachers receive some compensation for their extra efforts; we suggest that the principal consider rebalancing the duty schedule or providing compensatory time in exchange.

Scheduling

We recommend that staffing meetings be conducted approximately four times a year. Some schools have systems in place for collecting formative assessment data. For example, many middle schools use interim reports, high schools generally have scheduled examinations, and elementary schools often administer mid-year reading inventories. Schools with these systems in place should revise our suggested schedule to coincide with the availability of these data.

The first staffing meeting typically is scheduled several weeks prior to the end of the first grading period, which also is usually several weeks prior to parent-teacher conferences. Consequently, this permits teachers to discuss student concerns with their peers and plan interventions, which then can be shared with parents during conference time. It is much better to say to parents, "Mary's having a problem in mathematics, and here's the plan we have devised to help her," than it is to just confront parents with the problem.

The second set of staffings often is scheduled at the end of the first semester. The third is held prior to the end of the third nine-week grading period (or during the fifth six-week grading period). This places the third staffing meeting prior to possible spring parent-teacher conferences. Both of these meetings are important for monitoring students' progress and adjusting instructional pacing and approaches.

The primary purpose of the final staffing, which generally is conducted after the students have departed at the end of the school year, is to use summative data from both classroom and large-scale assessments to summarize the performance of the past year's students and plan for the coming year.

Typical staffing meetings last approximately 1½ to 2 hours. If all meetings were conducted after school, the burden on teachers would be great. We argue that there are other after-school meetings that can be dispensed with to make room for these important gatherings. A variety of approaches can be used to provide time for staffings. For instance, it often is possible to schedule a staffing meeting for part of a teacher workday or professional development day. Once a year, funds may be available to provide substitutes for the participating teachers, so that that meeting may be held during normal school hours. Figure 4.1 suggests a two-day schedule when substitutes are available. The principal also may forgo the monthly faculty meeting to allow time after school for staffings. The final staffing of the year generally is conducted after students leave for summer vacation.

Figure 4.1. Substitute Schedule for
Teachers Involved in Staffing Meeting

	Substitute 1	Substitute 2	Substitute 3	Substitute 4
Day 1				
Kindergarten Staffing				
8:00–10:00 A.M.	Cover Kindergarten Teacher A's Class	Cover Kindergarten Teacher B's Class	Cover Kindergarten Teacher C's Class	Cover Kindergarten Teacher D's Class
Grade 1 Staffing				
10:00–12:00 P.M.	Cover First Grade Teacher A's Class	Cover First Grade Teacher B's Class	Cover First Grade Teacher C's Class	Cover First Grade Teacher D's Class
Grade 2 Staffing				
12:30–2:30 P.M.	Cover Second Grade Teacher A's Class	Cover Second Grade Teacher B's Class	Cover Second Grade Teacher C's Class	Cover Second Grade Teacher D's Class
Day 2				
Grade 3 Staffing				
8:00–10:00 A.M.	Cover Third Grade Teacher A's Class	Cover Third Grade Teacher B's Class	Cover Third Grade Teacher C's Class	Cover Third Grade Teacher D's Class
Grade 4 Staffing				
10:00–12:00 P.M.	Cover Fourth Grade Teacher A's Class	Cover Fourth Grade Teacher B's Class	Cover Fourth Grade Teacher C's Class	Cover Fourth Grade Teacher D's Class
Grade 5 Staffing				
12:30–2:30 P.M.	Cover Fifth Grade Teacher A's Class	Cover Fifth Grade Teacher B's Class	Cover Fifth Grade Teacher C's Class	Cover Fifth Grade Teacher D's Class

Materials

A variety of information and materials must be available at the staffing. Core teachers bring pacing guides, grade books, planning books, student work samples, and any formative assessment results that are available. Teachers of students with special needs bring information regarding their students including their Individualized Education Programs (IEPs). Information about students from child study teams, teacher assistance teams, or roundtable meetings is helpful to have on hand. Specialty teachers bring grade books and any anecdotal records they may have compiled regarding their students' progress. The principal provides longitudinal data regarding student performance and the minutes of previous staffing meetings. Depending upon the focus of the meeting, a variety of other curriculum materials may be useful, including the following: curriculum guides, formative assessments, and a listing of test objectives.

Minutes

Minutes are kept for every staffing meeting. If possible, we suggest that a clerical staff member be assigned the task of recording and distributing minutes; otherwise, the administrator or department chair in attendance assumes this responsibility. Minutes are distributed to all personnel in attendance and all teachers who work with the students who have been discussed. In addition, we suggest that a cumulative notebook of agendas and minutes be maintained for each staffing group and stored in the principal's office. Care should be taken to protect confidentiality in the use and storage of these documents. To facilitate the easy distribution of minutes, the format can be customized by creating a word processing template for each group. Including a small box in the corner of the form that lists the names of all staff members to whom the minutes are to be distributed simplifies this process.

What Takes Place During Staffing Meetings?

The agenda of staffing meetings will vary depending upon the level of schooling and the time of the year. In the next section of this chapter, we suggest specific key questions that can be used to formulate agendas for staffing meetings that occur near the beginning, in the middle, and at the end of the school year. Most staffing meetings, however, include some if not all of the following agenda items.

Follow-up on Previous Recommendations

The first order of business in any staffing is a review of the recommendations made at the previous staffing. Following up on plans made for instructional interventions is key to establishing the credibility of the process. The surest way to short-circuit staffing meetings is to ignore the recommendations agreed upon by the group. It is the principal's responsibility to ensure that this does not happen. This is the time during which the group collectively evaluates the success of instructional interventions and decides whether or not specific efforts are to be continued.

Review Formative Assessment Data

Teachers review any available assessment data that describe student progress toward learning goals. If teachers were to review the pacing guide without related assessment information, they would know what was taught but not what was learned. Information about students' learning gives teachers feedback about the results of their planning and teaching.

Review Progress of Instructional Pacing

The next task is to review the instructional pace of courses and compare this to students' progress as indicated by formative assessment data. At the elementary school level, teachers review progress in language arts and reading, mathematics, science, and social studies. At the middle and high school levels, teachers of the same course (e.g., seventh grade social studies or Algebra II/Trig.) work together. Regardless of level, teachers discuss the overall pace of instruction and suggest revisions in this year's pacing plan if warranted.

Identify Individuals or Small Groups of Students Who are not Progressing Sufficiently and Plan Instructional Interventions

As a normal outgrowth of the review of pacing guides, teachers identify students who do not comprehend the content at the same pace as other students. A different approach to curriculum and/or some kind of instructional intervention may be necessary for these students. Responsibility for seeing that any changes are implemented must be clearly assigned to an individual teacher, counselor, or administrator. A variety of suggestions for approaches to curriculum and instructional interventions will be offered later in this chapter and in Chapter 5.

Follow-up

When recommendations and decisions are made in staffing meetings, teachers must be diligent about planning how they will be implemented and who will be responsible for doing so. All of us have attended meetings in which wonderful ideas were discussed and plans were made and then never heard of again. The follow-up component of staffing meetings requires a frequent review of previous minutes, revisiting of decisions, and monitoring the implementation of those decisions. Ideally, this follow-up is the responsibility of the team as a collaborative group. In some cases, the team assigns the monitoring responsibility to one or two members (see the sample agendas shown in Figures 4.2, on the next page, and 4.3, p. 64).

How Do Staffing Meetings Change as the Year Progresses?

The **first staffing** meeting of the year focuses on how the pacing guide, which was prepared before school started, "fits" the population of students now in our classes. Although it is held very early in the school year, teachers have begun to collect assessment information on individual students, and they may also have access to information from the previous spring about the achievement of these students. By now, most teachers will also have enough experience with their classes to know how they will need to adjust the general pace of instruction for the year. They will have identified students who may need opportunities for enrichment or acceleration, as well as students who will need extra help in order to meet the expectations of the course or grade level. Armed with this information, teachers discuss the current needs of students and review their pacing guides with an eye to matching the pace of instruction to the abilities of the students.

The following key questions can serve as a guide for developing the agenda for the year's first staffing meeting:

- What have we learned about these students' skills, abilities, and learning styles (both individuals and groups)?

- What early indications do we have about adjustments that may need to be made to our pacing guides?

- What regrouping, review, different approaches to curriculum, or other interventions can we implement now to help students who appear to be falling behind?

The **second and third staffing** meetings take place well into the school year. By now, teachers will know the achievement levels of their students in a variety of areas. They will have collected classroom assessment information about what students have learned and about their current academic needs. Depending on the timing of district or state-level testing, this type of data may be available as well.

(Text continues on page 65.)

Figure 4.2. Third Grade Staffing Agenda Date: 3/15/2003

Professionals Included: Third grade teachers Jones, Smith, and Black; Title I teacher Green; Special Education teacher Charles; music teacher Bach; art teacher Monet; PE teacher Jordan; guidance counselor Freud; Principal Williams; and secretary Paige.

Follow-up on Previous Suggestions (from 11/2/02 meeting):

1. Speed pace for social studies instruction.
2. Regroup John, Paul, Ringo, and George for specific skills instruction in reading comprehension.
3. Find a math tutor for Mary, Olivia, and Ben.
4. Increase scheduled time for SS; reduce scheduled time for SCI.

Review Formative Assessment Data:

Review Instructional Pacing:
   Language arts/Reading:

   Mathematics:

   Social Studies:

   Science:

Revise Pacing Guides:

Identify Individual and Small Group Needs for Instructional Intervention or Enrichment:

Figure 4.3. Math Department Staffing Agenda Date: 3/15/2003

Professionals Included: Math teachers Heinlein, Clarke, Farmer, Pournelle, Niven, Bradbury, Asimov, Wells, Einstein, Kepler, and Newton; special education teacher Charles; ESL teacher Jones; guidance counselor Freud; Assistant Principal Lopez; and secretary Paige.

Follow-up on Previous Suggestions (from 11/2/02 meeting):

1. Find tutors for Asimov's 5 struggling students in Algebra I, Part 2, (Freud).

2. Get software in lab working (Lopez).

3. Regroup Einstein and Kepler's third block Geometry classes for one week of intervention and enrichment based upon next quarterly assessment (Einstein and Kepler).

4. Redo AP Calculus pacing guide, falling behind (Newton).

Review Formative Assessment Data:

Review Instructional Pacing:
     Algebra I:

     Algebra II:

     Geometry:

     Math Analysis:

     College Algebra and Trig:

     AP Calculus:

Revise Pacing Guides:

Identify Individual and Small Group Needs for Instructional Intervention or Enrichment:

In addition to these student data, teachers will be able to discuss the general progress of each class as it compares to the pacing guide. Some groups and individuals will be further along or will have studied a unit in greater depth than was planned. In other cases, classes or groups of students may be progressing at a slower pace than the pacing guide indicates. Teachers in both of these meetings have the assessment data they need to identify needed adjustments in pacing and instruction. The following key questions can serve as a guide for developing agendas for these mid-year meetings:

♦ Are assessments providing sufficient and meaningful information to make good decisions regarding each student's program? If not, what assessments need to be added or changed?

♦ What do our daily and unit assessments suggest about students' likely performance on upcoming large-scale tests?

♦ Which students need review, remediation, other approaches to curriculum, and/or other instruction interventions, and how will they get this assistance?

♦ Do any of our data reveal a pattern of the group's performance that suggests needed changes in the pacing guide?

The year's **final staffing** meeting occurs either close to or after the end of the school year. In this meeting, teachers on the team have the opportunity to compare their assessments of student achievement to the results of large-scale assessments. This is also an opportunity, before departing for several weeks, to review the entire year's plan and make notes about revisions to be made the following year. The following key questions can serve as a guide for developing an agenda:

♦ To what extent did the results of our classroom assessments reflect the results of the large-scale assessments?

♦ In analyzing students' subtest results from large-scale assessments, what can we determine about the group's strengths and weaknesses?

♦ In analyzing our data by subgroups of students, do we find achievement gaps among racial, economic, or other groups?

♦ What information about these students' performance will be useful to their next teachers, and how will we share it with them?

♦ What changes should be made to our pacing guides, assessments, and instructional and curricular approaches for next year to address concerns revealed in these data?

Staffing meetings that are held regularly and have carefully planned agendas are a mechanism for an ongoing dialogue about student progress. Analysis of assessment data keeps the conversation focused on performance, and the structure provided by the pacing guide provides a vehicle for looking back and planning ahead.

How Can Potential Roadblocks Be Anticipated and Overcome?

Sometimes faculties find it difficult to get periodic staffing meetings up and running in their schools. Discomfort with this process can occur for a variety of reasons, but in our experience the two main causes are teachers' lack of experience working in teams and the absence of leadership.

Teachers' Ability and Experience Working in Teams

First, many groups of teachers have little or no experience working as collaborative teams. The importance of a collaborative culture and process in a school cannot be overstated if we expect teachers to take collective responsibility for the achievement of students. Collaboration is difficult to build in schools, as the isolated "one teacher in each classroom" model continues to be the predominant organizational structure. Given the physical environment and the schedules in which they work, it is common for teachers to spend days (and sometimes weeks) without substantive interaction with colleagues.

Attention to the Process by the Principal

For collaboration to be effective and meaningful, principals must attend to both the *structure* and *content* of the teams' staffing meeting discussions. By *structures* we mean factors such as schedules, material and clerical resources, and leadership, which create the potential for teams to make decisions collaboratively. Schedules of team members must include regular times for the team's work to be accomplished, such as common planning periods or regular times before or after school (but within contract hours). Resources must be available that make it possible for teams to work as efficiently and effectively as possible. The resources that teams need vary, of course, according to the kind of planning and decision making they do. At the very least, essentials such as space, multiple copies of curriculum guides and materials, computers, and clerical support must be provided. When principals take the initiative to organize time within the workday for meetings, allocate adequate space, and arrange for clerical support, the potential for teamwork is enhanced.

For this potential to be realized, leaders must also pay attention to the *content* of staffing meetings. By *content* we refer to the topics of discussion during the staffing meeting. We believe the content of the staffing meeting should include the following:

- Discussions regarding general curriculum pacing,
- The analysis of the results of formative assessment designed to measure how groups and individuals are learning,
- The selection of appropriate approaches to curriculum, and
- The development of instructional interventions.

The discussion must be focused around key questions that connect student achievement and needs to the pacing guide. Meaningful decisions must be made that have an obvious impact on student achievement. By using the pacing guide as a centerpiece, and by organizing agendas around these key questions, leaders are able to focus the conversation of the group on important instructional decisions that have a direct connection to student learning. When teams of teachers come together for a staffing meeting, they must focus on the connection between instruction and student learning, by examining their own pacing guides, identifying areas for change, and sharing responsibility for making those changes work for students. Although veering away from the agenda to discuss other important topics may be acceptable occasionally, it is wise to limit such excursions, primarily because they extend the meeting and/or detract from the central purpose of the staffing.

Availability of Appropriate Intervention Resources

If teachers are charged, as they often are in staffing meetings, with the task of planning instructional interventions for students, they need to be aware of the resources available. Will they be able to extend the school day for some students? Do IEP meetings need to be reconvened to alter the amount of time a student receives special education services or to identify additional supports and accommodations? Are paraprofessionals or volunteers available to help as tutors? Can alternative textbooks or text sets of multilevel tradebooks be purchased for students at various reading levels? Principals must be clear at the outset of the staffing process as to what resources, and consequently what interventions, are available, so that teams know the parameters within which they can make decisions.

Opportunities to Communicate
Across Departments and Grade Levels

Another barrier to effective staffing meetings—probably an effect of the isolation described earlier—is that teachers have too few occasions to discuss and gain information about the achievement of students schoolwide. Most teachers have a high degree of concern about how their own students are doing, but the pressures of time and the huge responsibilities of their jobs get in the way of their learning about the progress of students in other courses and other grades. When faced with data describing the achievement of groups of students other than their own, some teachers are reluctant to contribute ideas and make suggestions. "It's like looking in someone else's purse," one teacher was heard to say. A culture in which students in the school are "everyone's kids" is hard to achieve in the face of such attitudes. One remedy for such grade-level/subject isolation has been described previously. During the process of creating the pacing guides we emphasized the need to conduct articulation meetings with other grade levels to identify gaps and redundancy in the curriculum. It also is advisable to conduct cross–grade-level meetings to analyze longitudinal summative assessment data for groups of students as they progress through elementary school; middle school; or the mathematics, English, history, or science department throughout the high school years.

Sample Strategies that Might Emerge from Staffing Meeting Discussion

What do you do when a student or a group of students is not mastering material as prescribed on the pacing guide? This question alone is worth a thousand-page book. Chapter 5 will describe a process and several strategies for planning and modifying instruction for students. In this section we briefly describe a variety of instructional alterations and interventions that might be considered in response to the preceding question.

The range of modifications is nearly endless, and when groups of teachers agree to use a common curriculum, to follow a common pacing guide, administer common formative assessments, and collaboratively monitor student progress, the possibilities for instructional intervention increase dramatically. One of the keys is to plan collaboratively for some of these interventions to reduce the workload for individual teachers and promote instructional consistency for students.

Regrouping Students

One method for addressing students' weaknesses is to temporarily regroup them based on reteaching needs. Two or more teachers who teach the same content during the same time period, who pace at the same rate, and who gather common assessment data, may decide to regroup their students for a short time period of time based upon identified deficits and strengths. After this period of remediation and enrichment, the original groupings can be reconstituted. (For an example of this using Algebra I, see Rettig & Canady, 1998).

Other options for regrouping can be used when general classroom and special teachers co-teach. Co-teaching draws on the unique strengths of both teachers and enables two teachers to assume various complementary roles depending on the instructional purpose. There are five co-teaching models: (1) one teaching, one supporting; (2) station teaching; (3) parallel teaching; (4) alternative teaching; and (5) team teaching (Friend and Cook, 1996). These various formats are underutilized and often replaced by an ineffective scenario of the general education teacher assuming the major teaching responsibilities and the special educator merely monitoring instruction or assisting as needed. An example of using co-teaching to provide needed review or enrichment involves alternative teaching. Here the class is divided into two unequal groups—the larger group reviews or does an enrichment activity, while the smaller group has concepts retaught, a lesson previewed, or a specific skill reemphasized. Either teacher may work with either group, although it is important to vary the composition of the groups and rotate the teachers to avoid stigma. Another effective way to coteach involves station teaching. Here the students are divided into three groups, and they rotate among three sections of the room. One teacher provides a direct instruction lesson, the second teacher provides another direct instruction lesson, and a third station requires independent work. Implementation of these models leads to a less fragmented and more contextualized curriculum for students with special needs and provides greater instructional intensity and engaged time in the general education classroom (Friend & Cook, 1996).

Changing Placement

It may be necessary at times to change a student's placement to a faster- or slower-moving group in an elementary school or to higher- or lower-course level in middle or high school. For example, an elementary student may have just finished an intense series of *Reading Recovery* sessions, and have progressed dramatically in reading level. It would be wise to move this student to a group on his/her instructional level. Similarly, a student who is failing Algebra I might be moved to an Algebra I, Part I, class after all other interventions have proven ineffective. We regard a downward change of placement as a last resort after all other efforts have failed.

Providing More Time to Learn

All educators know that students learn at different rates, yet we persist in allowing time to be the constant and the amount of learning to be the variable in our educational equations. At times it is more appropriate to allow additional time to learn (with diagnosis of weaknesses and intense instruction applied) than to permit a student to go on without the basic skills necessary to succeed.

All too often this is seen in high school mathematics. A student struggles early in algebra class, but the show must go on because most students have grasped the basic content. As the teacher and the class press forward, the struggling student falls further and further behind until comprehension of new topics is impossible. Failure is now certain. If only that student could have been given more time to learn the basic concepts.

There are a variety of ways to provide students with more time to learn. Summer school has been the American standard for students who need more time, although most secondary students who attend do so because they have failed a course. If more learning time is the issue (rather than behavioral issues that often are the real cause of failure), why not assign an "incomplete" and use summer school to provide more time? This change in school culture recognizes the need for additional learning time and an "incomplete" provides a more optimistic message to students than a failing grade.

Of course, we would prefer to provide more learning time before it becomes too late. This would involve finding additional time during the original course of instruction. One could ask the student to come after school, during lunchtime, or during a study hall to receive additional assistance. Some schools offer "Saturday School," where students get attendance credit as well as academic help. As any teacher knows, each of these means of providing students more time has its problems. Students (and teachers, for that matter) often are loath to meet after school. Lunchtime is much too short to use for academic assistance in most schools. A student's study hall period most likely would not match the teacher's availability, which would mean receiving help from a teacher other than the one who originally taught the material (although in some cases this might be a plus). School on Saturday generally is anathema to both students and teachers unless paid or coerced, although we are aware of a high school that operates a voluntary Saturday School from 8:30–11:30 A.M. each week. Neither students nor faculty are required to attend. Students report to the auditorium, and the teachers present that day announce what they will be teaching. Students then choose their teachers for the morning and move to classrooms. Using the pacing guides available for each course, teachers review the previous week's work. Students receive attendance credit and are able to replace a quiz or classwork grade with one assigned by their Saturday School teacher for their efforts that morning. After two years of operation, a typical Saturday will find 400 students and 40 teachers participating.

The school schedule also can be designed to offer students more time to learn. A typical method is to track students into a section of a course that has been paced more slowly. The most common example of this is the division that often is made of Algebra I into Algebra I, Part 1, and Algebra I, Part 2. Rather than completing the entire course in one year; two years are allocated. In the 4/4 high school block schedule, in which students complete four full-year courses each semester, this is accomplished in one year by teaching Algebra I, Part 1, first semester every day for 90 minutes, and Algebra I, Part 2, second semester. In an A/B block schedule, Algebra I meets every day, all year long, for 90 minutes, rather than every other day, like most other courses. (For a detailed discussion of these scheduling formats, see Canady and Rettig, 1995.)

Unfortunately, the method just described requires school staff to decide on a student's track before they even begin the course. However, the schedule can be adapted in more creative ways. For example, what if we schedule three (or more) sections of Algebra I during the same period or block? Each teacher follows the same pacing guide. At the end of the first nine weeks a common assessment is administered to all three sections. At the staffing meeting a discussion occurs regarding the results of this assessment, and students are regrouped among the teachers. Perhaps two-thirds of the students have mastered the concepts of the first nine weeks sufficiently to move on; they are regrouped with two of the teachers. The third teacher remediates the weaknesses identified by the assessments with the help of a special education teacher and the math specialist from the district office. Consequently, this teacher changes the instructional pace for these students. They may need more time at the end of the term to complete the course. Every nine weeks the process is repeated (for a detailed description of the schedules and processes that support this idea, see Rettig & Canady, 2000; Rettig & Canady, 1998).

Using the Computer Lab in Creative Ways

Typically, when a computer lab is used to support instruction the teacher escorts her entire class to the lab to engage in a practice activity or project of some sort. We offer another alternative, which provides support for what we know to be good practice. Using the pacing guide, the teacher plans four days of instruction. Near the end of the fourth instructional period or block, she administers a short quiz designed to measure mastery of the concepts taught during the past four days. Based upon the results of the quiz, she divides her class into "those who got it" (the enrichment group) and "those who need help" (the reteaching group). On the fifth day she works with the reteaching group, approximately half of her class, and she provides instruction and activities based upon the weaknesses identified in the quiz. Her enrichment group travels to the computer lab, where they use software that reinforces and broadens their understanding of the same concepts. Most likely half of another class also is in the lab. Because the software utilized is keyed to the skill levels of individual users and records their progress for the teacher to review at a later time, the other group could be from a different class or even subject. The lab is supervised by a teacher, or perhaps more economically, by a paraprofessional trained to keep the lab up and running. On the sixth day the groups switch venues, and the teacher provides an enrichment activity while students in the reteaching group use software, which provides practice and reinforcement of the retaught concepts. The cycle is then repeated with four days of instruction, an assessment, and then two days of reteaching or enrichment. The schedule obviously requires a computer lab with appropriate software and supervision, but it would serve many teachers and students and would institutionalize practice that we know to be effective. (For a more detailed description of this scheduling model see Rettig & Canady, 2000, Chap. 7).

Modifying the Pacing Guide

It may be determined from the formative assessment data discussed in the staffing meeting that more than just a few students are having difficulty maintaining the instructional pace set by the teacher. In this case it will be necessary to alter the pacing guide. The entire group may need reteaching of certain concepts. Topics scheduled for later in the school year may need to be omitted or abbreviated. Regardless, the staffing team should work together to redesign the plan for instruction.

Approaching the Curriculum from a Different Angle

Sometimes by approaching the curriculum from a different angle, we can allow more students to be successful in meeting high standards. Several of these approaches have been described previously in the literature on gifted and special education (Polloway & Patton, 1993; Torrance & Sisk, 1999). We have adapted this work by combining a number of options and developing a planning guide (Figure 4.4, p. 74), which illustrates that one or more approaches may be used in a complementary manner as teachers plan to meet students' needs. There are two broad types of curricula provided for students in school. The vast majority of students can benefit from the general, *developmental* curriculum, which has its foundation in national and state standards and is based on the premise that mastery of objectives is a prerequisite for moving to the next higher level. For example, math skills build sequentially, and students need to know about numbers and basic operations prior to moving to more complex skills like multiplication of fractions. In direct contrast, a *functional* curriculum is required for a specific population of students with more severe disabilities who need to acquire a limited set of critical skills essential for living and working. Students who need direct instruction to learn to care for their personal needs, balance a checkbook, acquire basic job skills, or access community resources are in a this specialized curriculum. While not always the case, this functional approach usually replaces a developmental curriculum. These students generally are exempt from standardized state assessments; alternate functional assessments are substituted. In this section we will focus on students who are appropriately placed in a developmental or general education curriculum, yet would benefit from accessing this curriculum from a slightly different approach.

Several approaches can benefit students for whom mastery of the developmental curriculum will not be difficult. A *compacted* approach acknowledges that certain students already may have mastered some of the developmental curriculum, and they should be provided with opportunities to progress more rapidly through basic objectives. For example, when students score well on a pretest in spelling or science, they move forward to new material rather than repeat what they already know. These students may then benefit from either an enriched or accelerated curriculum. An *enrichment* approach provides more depth and elaboration of developmental curriculum objectives. The curriculum content remains the same, but students explore a topic more extensively and gain additional understanding. This may take the form of alternative or extended examples, activities, or problems. While working on the same history objectives, some students may conduct research to explore a topic beyond what their peers are doing and what the basic curriculum prescribes. With an *accelerated* approach the teacher provides advanced curriculum not typically assigned to the students' grade level. For example, students who demonstrate mastery of math objectives often are moved ahead to study algebra in eighth (or even seventh grade) rather than ninth grade, where Algebra I is traditionally offered.

Students for whom mastery of the developmental curriculum may be challenging can be aided by other approaches that provide curriculum access. In a *remedial* approach to curriculum specific basic skill deficits are targeted for improvement. Students typically receive intensive instruction in reading, writing, and/or mathematics. It is critical to remediate reading difficulties as reading significantly impacts the learners' performance on all high stakes tests. The teacher provides direct instruction, and the student actively works to enhance these weaker skills to be able to benefit fully from the developmental curriculum. Schools generally have a variety of personnel assigned to provide such specialized instruction to students. Common programs are special education, Title I, English as a Second Language (ESL), remedial reading or mathematics, Book Buddies, and tutors.

Another approach involves *compensatory* measures. In certain learning situations, the student's skill deficits might be ignored in favor of finding ways to compensate for these weaknesses. For example, a student with severe spelling difficulties who is working on a science project might use a spell checker. The student might also have reading problems and use a talking pen to scan printed words or a tape recorder to listen to books. This is not to say that the spelling or reading problems should not continue to be remediated, but in some learning situations it might be advantageous to circumvent weaknesses so the student can master content area curriculum objectives. This is especially true for students with skill deficits in language arts or English, who are placed in content science, social studies, or math classes.

Figure 4.4. Selection of Curriculum Types
& Approaches Planning Guide

Student(s):		Date:
Directions: ✔ the appropriate curriculum types and approaches		
____**Developmental Curriculum** (spiraling general curriculum; each step is prerequisite for next more complex level)	____**Functional Curriculum** (basic life skills)	
Curriculum Approach	*Notes & Details*	*Teacher(s) & Roles*
____**Compacted** (instruction for only unmastered skills)		
____**Enrichment** (elaboration & extension of general curriculum)		
____**Accelerated** (advanced curriculum)		
____**Remedial** (improvement of basic skill deficits)		
____**Compensatory** (alternatives to compensate for weaknesses)		
____**Learning Strategy** (sequential strategic steps)		
____**Tutorial** (assistance for studying, assignments & projects as needed)		
____**Integrated** (cross-disciplinary curriculum integration)		

Learning strategies, another approach to consider, focuses on providing students with strategic steps for accomplishing multistep learning tasks. For example, a student who does not proofread well might be taught to follow a sequence of specific steps and self-monitor performance or a multistep strategy might help a student accurately complete word problems in mathematics. Minskoff and Allsopp (2003) provide additional information on the learning strategies approach and details regarding use at the Learning Toolbox website at http://coe.jmu.edu/learningtoolbox.

A *tutorial* approach involves assisting individual students by assigning a tutor. This role can be assumed by a volunteer, paraprofessional, or even another student who is the same age or an older peer. We believe the role of tutor is generally not an effective use of the professional expertise of a special educator. Care must be taken to schedule these one-on-one sessions at times that do not conflict with other courses and where the assignment of a tutor will not be seen as punishment. Tutoring allows a student to obtain assistance as needed for whatever tasks are currently required in the general education classroom. The student and teacher might prepare for an upcoming test, work on a book report, go over homework, or complete unfinished classroom activities. This approach generally solves an immediate academic crisis and boosts grades but may offer little in terms of long-lasting skills or knowledge.

Finally, an *integrated* approach to curriculum has the potential to facilitate the learning of all students. Here, curricula from various content areas are integrated into a thematic instructional unit. This approach often highlights natural curricular connections and reinforces prior learning. For example, a social studies teacher who designed a theme-based unit, such as The Great Depression, would then integrate skills or activities in other subject areas like music, math, or literature with this topic. This approach may allow gifted students to go far beyond the requirements of the developmental curriculum and struggling learners to make connections that facilitate the acquisition of basic curriculum objectives.

These approaches to curriculum may appear to be somewhat artificial, yet they facilitate very pragmatic consideration about what different students need in various educational environments. It is likely that individuals or groups of students will require combinations of these approaches to demonstrate achievement of curriculum standards. Classroom teachers, special education teachers, other support specialists, families, and students, if appropriate, must work together to choose complementary approaches to curriculum. The chart in Figure 4.4 will enable teachers at an instructional planning, staffing, or IEP meeting to efficiently and effectively facilitate the identification of appropriate curriculum approaches and establish roles for those professionals working with the student. As the team begins, they should consider each of the curriculum approaches and check off those that are applicable to the particular student or group of students. Specific details related to instruction or materials are placed in the second column, and then the roles and responsibilities of individual teachers or instructional support personnel can be listed in the third column. This relatively quick process will assist educators in considering the range of available options and not limiting themselves to only one or two possibly ineffective approaches. Making these decisions will also enable educators to see how they can collaborate with each other by focusing on mutually agreed upon goals.

Modifying Instruction

Perhaps the most powerful instructional intervention we can make is to change the methods we use to teach and/or reteach our students. There often are surprising and positive results when alternative instructional approaches are applied to content students have had difficulty learning. Chapter 5 is devoted to this important topic.

Conclusion

Constructing pacing guides, although a useful and instructive task, creates yet another paper document to which teachers should refer. As teachers are inundated with dozens of such documents yearly, it is not surprising that many receive only cursory attention. How can we ensure that our carefully constructed guides are used as intended? The creation of a collaborative learning community with regularly scheduled staffing meetings, as a key part of that organizational structure, is our best answer.

5

Creating Pacing Guides: The Instructional Phase

Chapter 5 is designed to help teachers plan "learner-friendly" instruction through the use of a five-step strategy called the IEP-DR, which encourages the teacher to simultaneously consider both the needs of students and the demands of instructional tasks to predict potential problems students may face in the classroom and then to plan instruction accordingly.

We make five assumptions before we move on to the process described in this chapter:

- ◆ First, the teacher possesses the appropriate level of content knowledge.

- ◆ Second, the curriculum is aligned with the standards.

- ◆ Third, the teacher is using a pacing guide to plan and monitor instruction (Chapter 2).

- ◆ Fourth, assessment is closely linked to the curriculum (Chapter 3).

- ◆ Fifth, student progress is monitored on an ongoing basis (Chapter 4).

All of these components must be in place for students to attain full access to the curriculum. Students with special needs, however, often encounter instructional barriers that limit or prohibit them from achieving their full potential.

Using the IEP-DR

Once an appropriate curriculum approach is selected (Chapter 4), it is important for educators to develop a systematic process for thinking about accommodating student needs at a more micro level. The IEP-DR is a five-step problem-solving process designed to help teachers predict the difficulties students might have in a specific learning situation and prevent or solve these problems (Figure 5.1). The first step asks the teacher to *identify the learning strengths and needs* of student(s) in the classroom. These include both academic skills (e.g., reading below grade level) and how a student works on academic tasks (e.g., organizational difficulties). Second, it is necessary to *evaluate the demands of the task* or classroom activity carefully. The teacher must consider the expectations for students' performance and evaluate exactly what the students must do to successfully complete the task. This step requires thoughtful analysis of task demands including directions, response modes, structure, and so forth. A critical third step is for the teacher to *predict potential problems* students will have with the task as it is currently designed. If the teacher does not change the task in any way, what problems will most likely occur as students attempt to complete it? Finally, once good teachers predict potential difficulties, they *develop modifications* in the task to accommodate learners. As a rule of thumb, the task should be modified as little as possible while still providing the maximum opportunity for learner success. Many activities can be altered in relatively minor ways, whereas some activities or tasks will require more substantial changes to facilitate success. Later, analysis of the students' performance on the completed task may indicate how the teacher should *revise as needed*. Often student responses will suggest improvements to be made when the task is used in the future: directions to be clarified, additional structure to be provided, or the addition of missing steps in the process. The task is adjusted to maximize learner success.

This problem-solving strategy can be applied to a wide range of typical classroom tasks, many of which pose difficulties for students with exceptional needs.

Figure 5.1. IEP-DR: A Strategy for Modifying Instruction

Identify students' needs and strengths

Evaluate the demands of the classroom task

Predict potential problems students may have

Develop modifications in the task

Revise as needed

Setting the Stage for the IEP-DR

First Staffing Meeting

When the social studies teachers revisited their pacing guides in early October, they were thankful they had taken time in August to use the state department resource guide that outlined the specific objectives of the curriculum in greater detail. Now that they were more confident about the content behind the curriculum objectives, they realized that the *reading level* of both the text and critical supplementary material was a problem for a group of students. In addition to reading, they expected students to be able to *take notes* both from the text and from information presented in class. These notes were important for studying for unit tests and exams. Unfortunately, when the teachers reviewed the notes of some of these students, they realized how *incomplete, illegible, and sometimes inaccurate* the notes were. With reading and note taking difficulties, no wonder these students were performing poorly on the end-of-unit assessments. They brainstormed strategies to try and help these students.

Staffing meetings, as described in Chapter 4, provide a structured forum for educators to monitor students' learning, identify these barriers to progress, and adjust instruction based on student needs. During staffings, students' difficulties can be identified and solutions sought. This does not mean that *every* need of *every* child is monitored and accommodated, but it does mean that a variety of effective techniques can be employed to adapt instruction and create a learner-friendly instructional environment for all students. The following scenarios illustrate several common concerns teachers have regarding students with special learning needs that may arise in staffing meetings.

Second Staffing Meeting

In early December, teachers gathered for their scheduled staffing meeting. The science curriculum included a lot of interesting material to teach, but such an overwhelming *abundance of information* for the students to understand and remember. Although teachers knew that their students would not take a state science test at the end of the year, they felt responsible to assure their students had a firm foundation upon which to continue learning the spiraling science curriculum. In addition, they knew that specific material would be tested several years later. Some of the students couldn't even *remember specific facts* for the unit test so how would they ever demonstrate mastery in the future? Despite the fact that these students had been in school for several years already, it was evident that some of the students still had not mastered important *organizational skills*. They were receiving consistently *poor homework* grades. The teachers worked together to develop solutions to these instructional problems.

Third Staffing Meeting

In early March, the team met for their third staffing. All was on schedule according to their pacing guides, but they were concerned about progress of four or five students in each class. Even though the curriculum objectives had been covered, the teachers knew these students were struggling with the *amount of complex material* and the type of assignments that were required. Based upon informal questioning and feedback from students, the teachers knew that the material was a huge blur. The students were trying desperately to remember all the *details* and relate them to *larger concepts,* but it was just too much. These same students were often inconsistent and *not strategic* in their approach to *multistep tasks* such as proofreading. *Longer-range projects,* such as research reports or science projects, involving *multiple requirements spread over time,* were also problematic for these students and the resulting student products were difficult to grade. The staffing meeting was devoted to identifying ideas for modifying instruction.

IEP-DR, Step One: Identifying Students' Needs and Strengths

The students described in these scenarios are struggling to achieve the learning goals and objectives outlined in the curriculum standards. They may have identified disabilities, may not speak English as their primary language, may be cognitively delayed, may not have adequate support at home, or may be at risk for school failure for a variety of other reasons. Some of the students will have Individualized Education Programs (IEPs) or 504 Plans, and still others may have individual academic plans, a growing trend (Craft, 2002). Although these students certainly bring individual learning needs to the classroom, effective teachers recognize that many of these needs overlap and that interventions can be planned that meet the needs of several students simultaneously. We do not mean to oversimplify the origin or nature of complex individual learning problems, but instead we want to help teachers see that these difficulties often have similar characteristics. Whenever possible, teachers need to capitalize on strengths while modifying instruction to accommodate the characteristics noted in Figure 5.2 (p. 81).

Before we move on, we want to dispense with a common reaction of some teachers when confronted with a student with learning problems: "He would do better if he just tried harder." What may appear to be lack of motivation may

Figure 5.2. Characteristics of Students with Special Needs

Disorganized
Unstrategic in approach to tasks and lack
problem-solving skills
Difficulty staying focused on task
Difficulty with abstract, as opposed to,
concrete learning tasks
Lack of attention to detail
Impulsive approach to academic tasks
Difficulty identifying critical aspects of task
Unwilling to take academic risks
Poor memory/retention of knowledge and skills
Poor test taking skills
Lack experiences relating to academic content
Lack independent study skills
Difficulty generalizing skills
Difficulty expressing what they know
Lack confidence in academic abilities
Poor readers
Cognitively passive learners
Difficulty identifying essential versus
nonessential information
Poor spelling
Lack social skills and difficulty working in groups
Lack of understanding of the writing process
or specific writing skills
Difficulties with legibility and speed of handwriting
Poor note takers
Difficulty seeing the big picture and relationships among information
Need much repetition of material
Difficulty getting started, maintaining task persistence, or monitoring completion

actually be the inability to accomplish academic tasks despite a student's best intentions. These students often try, but they have unproductive and inefficient strategies that do not provide successful payoff for their efforts. Thus begins a cycle of frustration that often results in the student giving up. At the elementary level the student might legitimately say, "I can't do this," but repeated failure often turns into, "I won't do this," by the time students are in middle or high school. Because they are unable to complete the task as initially structured, what these older students really mean is, "I can't and I don't want to risk failure by trying." Repeated failure causes students to become "success deprived," a serious problem that negatively affects motivation. The IEP-DR can be used help plan instruction that will increase the chances of success for students struggling in a standards-based learning environment.

IEP-DR, Step Two: Evaluating the Demands of the Classroom Task

Equally important is the need to critically analyze the specific requirements of tasks or activities that are typically incorporated into daily or weekly instruction. Although the goal of the instructional tasks may be appropriate, the structure of the tasks may create major stumbling blocks for learners who are struggling. For example, students might be expected to do homework, comprehend content area reading material, take notes, remember essential information, complete projects, study, and take tests. The specific requirements of any one of these assignments could thwart the best effort of a student with special needs. Figure 5.3 highlights a variety of learning tasks in a typical classroom.

IEP-DR, Step Three: Predict Potential Problems

When teachers don't critically analyze the demands of specific classroom tasks and fail to understand the learning characteristics students bring to these tasks, they set up a recipe for failure. We strongly recommend that teachers develop the habit of predicting potential problems and then purposefully designing learner-friendly instruction that meets the needs of students with learning difficulties. Understanding the needs of learners is often not as easy as it seems because most teachers were successful in school themselves, and as learners they did not experience many of these problems. We cannot modify instruction effectively, however, unless we are able to predict the impact of these learning problems and develop appropriate solutions. Potential problems can be predicted by simultaneously considering the learners' needs and the requirements of the classroom task (Figure 5.4, p. 84).

Figure 5.3. Typical Learning Tasks

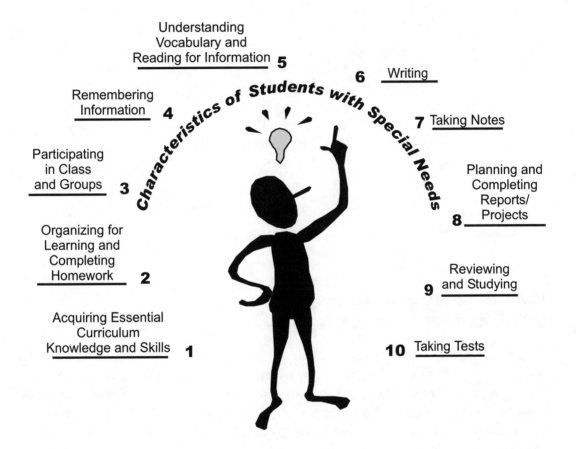

Figure 5.4. Identifying Potential Learning Problems

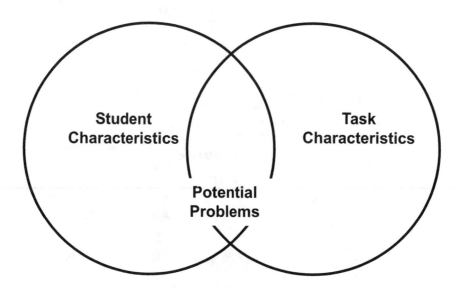

IEP-DR, Step Four: Develop Modifications in the Task

What can be done to help struggling learners? First, as highlighted in Chapter 4, we must select the most appropriate general curriculum tactic from among a variety of available approaches (see Figure 4.4, p. 74). Second, we must modify instructional tasks after carefully analyzing both students' learning needs and the attributes of learning tasks, and predicting potential learning problems.

One question we've often heard asked is, "Is it fair to provide something special or different for some students but not for everyone?" We believe the issue of fairness involves providing what students need. In many cases, instruction will be planned to accommodate specific learning needs, but everyone in the class will benefit. When a teacher provides a graphic organizer to facilitate students' comprehension and to develop a framework for learning, all students, not just those with learning difficulties benefit. Similarly, when a teacher provides (or the class creates) a mnemonic technique to facilitate remembering specific content, all students may benefit, also.

In other situations, modifications will be provided for specific groups or even individual students but not for all. In this case, only some students actually need the modification, and it would limit the progress or independence of other students to provide it for them, too. For example, a teacher may provide a structured note-taking guide to accommodate those students who have difficulty capturing information from an oral presentation, from notes written on the board or overhead projector, or from a textbook. Although some students may benefit from this practice because they are still developing their note-taking skills, others already may have acquired skills to an independent level. In another example, the teacher creates independent practice activities for those students who require additional repetition and interaction with the material. Others, who have already mastered the concepts, do not require this additional practice.

The questions that follow are designed to assist teachers in critically analyzing their instruction to design instructional modifications that maximize learner success within the context of everyday tasks and activities. The questions correspond to the typical classroom tasks that have been highlighted previously (see Figure 5.3, p. 83) and take into account learner characteristics (see Figure 5.2, p. 81). These are especially useful in initial planning of an instructional unit beginning with the identification of essential objectives and ending with assessment of student outcomes. We do not advocate that teachers fragment the curriculum into isolated bits and pieces but rather that teachers analyze the smaller components prior to integrating them into an instructional whole. This type of planning can be used effectively by either the general education classroom teacher of the specialist in an inclusive or pull-out setting.

Instructional Planning Prompts

Area 1: Acquiring Essential
Curriculum Knowledge and Skills

♦ What is the essential curriculum information, and how can I help students comprehend the overall framework?

♦ How can I help students see the relationships among information in the unit?

♦ What type of graphic format best fits the information?

♦ How can I model thinking aloud to promote higher order thinking skills?

♦ How can I provide multiple means of presentation of information?

♦ How can I scaffold knowledge and skills?

Area 2: Organizing for Learning
and Completing Homework

♦ How can I assist students in becoming organized to learn?

♦ How can I facilitate homework completion?

Area 3: Participating in Class and Groups

♦ How can I promote positive interdependence?

♦ How can I form and structure groups for maximum success?

♦ How can I promote individual accountability?

Area 4: Remembering Information

♦ What information must be remembered?

♦ What information will be difficult for students to remember?

♦ Which memory technique will help students remember information?

Area 5: Understanding Vocabulary
& Reading for Information

♦ What is the essential vocabulary for the unit?

♦ How can I make the vocabulary words come alive or become memorable?

♦ How can I promote deeper meaning of vocabulary?

♦ How can I help nonreaders compensate for inability to read the material?

♦ How can I provide below–grade-level readers with reading success?

♦ How can I enhance strategic reading skills?

♦ How can I prepare students prior to reading?

♦ What can I do during reading to promote success?

♦ What can I do after reading to promote comprehension?

Area 6: Writing

♦ How can I engage students in writing?

♦ How can I incorporate steps of the writing process?

♦ How can I provide explicit structure for the writing task?

♦ How can I help students generalize specific skills to writing?

♦ How can I encourage students to proofread effectively?

Area 7: Taking Notes

♦ How can I assist students in taking accurate and complete notes?

- How can I keep students actively involved during the presentation of information?

- How can I help students develop specific note taking skills?

Area 8: Planning and Completing Reports/Projects

- How can I explicitly provide purpose and directions for the activity?

- How can I help students understand the requirements of the task and how they will be evaluated?

- How can I break the task into sequential substeps?

- How can I provide examples of projects that meet, exceed, and don't meet expectations?

- How can I help students self-monitor accurate completion of steps?

Area 9: Reviewing and Studying

- How can I quickly assess student understanding of information?

- How can I actively involve all students in reviewing?

- How can I build fluency through varied in-class review activities?

- How can I provide a supportive environment for reviewing essential information?

- How can I actively involve students in independent practice?

- How can I vary the independent review strategies used within a unit?

- How can I include the way in which the information was learned or remembered?

- How can I use a student-friendly study guide to share essential curriculum information with students and families?

Area 10: Taking Tests

- How can I provide a range of question types?

- How can I incorporate questions at various cognitive levels?

- How can I incorporate a range of response modes?

- How can I use various approaches to grading?

- How can I provide effective feedback regarding student performance?

Figure 5.5 provides a number of possible strategies that teachers might use in responding to the instructional prompts listed in above.

Figure 5.5. Selected Strategies for Modifying Learning Tasks

- Establishment of meaningful purpose and links to prior knowledge
- Concrete learning before abstract concepts
- Explicit identification of essential information
- Organized, scaffolded, and structured information
- Tasks divided into sequential steps
- Big picture/ideas before the smaller details
- Illustration of informational relationships
- Demonstration, modeling, and think alouds
- Active involvement
- Scaffolded instruction to support learning
- Multiple checks for understanding
- Gradual transition to independence
- Problem solving strategies
- Memory hooks
- Repetition and distributed review
- Opportunities to promote generalization & transfer

IEP-DR, Step Five: Revise as Needed

As changes occur in students' needs and/or instructional tasks and as data are analyzed regarding students' performance, new and different problems may arise that require alternative strategies and modifications. The IEP-DR should be a responsive decision-making and design tool.

Conclusion

Access to, and progress in, the general curriculum are important aspects of three legislative mandates: the Individuals with Disabilities Education Act (1997), Section 504 of the Vocational Rehabilitation Act (1973), and the Elementary and Secondary Education Act (2001). Our approach to modifying tasks for learners with special needs is grounded in the principles of "universal design for learning," the key tenets of which are access, participation, and progress (Hitchcock, Meyer, Rose, & Jackson, 2002). Just as curb cuts, ramps, and automatic door openers provide physical access, "cognitive ramps" allow access to the curriculum (Kame'enui & Simmons, 1999). These cognitive ramps should be built-in rather than added as afterthoughts, and they should be *universal*, designed to benefit a range of individuals. Through these cognitive supports, instructional materials and activities are designed to allow learning goals to be achieved by individuals with differences in the abilities to see, hear, speak, move, read, write, understand English, attend, organize, engage, and remember (Orkwis & McLane, 1998). Universally designed instruction does not result in lowered expectations or watered-down instruction, but rather calls for multiple ways to access the curriculum and show mastery of content (United States Department of Education, 1999). As instructional designers, teachers consider how best to weave elements of teaching strategies, materials, response modes, and assessment into seamless instruction. As adapted from the 21st Annual Report to Congress, three guiding questions are the following:

♦ Does instruction include multiple means of *presentation* of curriculum content?

♦ Does instruction include multiple and flexible means of student *engagement or participation*?

♦ Does instruction include multiple means of student *responses?*

The real challenge for educators is to provide students with access to meaningful curriculum that is aligned with standards and provided through effective instruction. Figure 5.6 (p. 90) illustrates the ramp required provide curriculum access for all students.

Providing curriculum access is the responsibility of every teacher. Access occurs in day-to-day classroom activities and necessitates the thoughtful analysis of instruction. Most teachers use relatively predictable instructional formats and tasks. The teacher must take the learning needs of the students and proactively adapt tasks by considering the instructional input and response modes (Janney & Snell, 2000). These adaptations involve changing the way teachers teach and/or the way students practice or demonstrate learning. Initially, these may be purposeful adaptations, but eventually they will become a natural part of the teacher's skill repertoire and a constant in each subsequent unit

As illustrated in this chapter, there are many variables to consider when planning effective instruction to promote high quality achievement. First, teachers use their understanding of *student characteristics* and knowledge of *essential learning objectives* to select appropriate *curriculum approaches* that enable

Figure 5.6. Providing an Accessible Curriculum

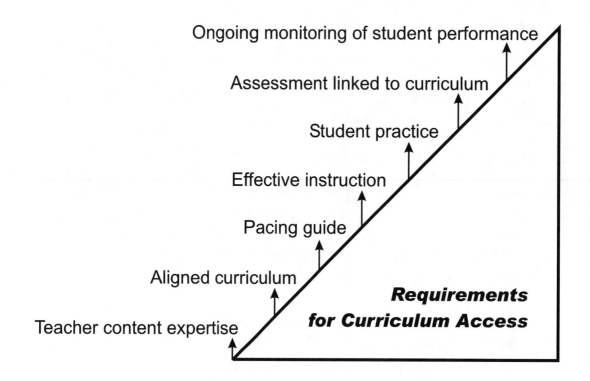

students to fully *access the curriculum* and to clarify *roles* of various educators. Second, effective teachers compare *student characteristics* with the demands of *typical instructional tasks* to proactively *predict potential problems*. Last, when developing an instructional unit, we encourage teachers to use *planning prompts* and the principles of *universal design* as they *develop modifications* which ultimately provide *curriculum access* for all learners.

6

Leading the Process at the School and District Levels

This chapter describes the important role of building level and district administrators in the curriculum design and implementation process. Although the processes may vary somewhat from district to district and school to school, we have identified a number of common factors that seem to be in place in school districts that have had success. We have found that these key elements are consistently present when a school or school district has achieved improved student test scores and overall school improvement. Although we realize that many of these factors have budgetary or financial considerations, we also believe that this fact should not deter the focused school or district from embarking on this journey.

Keys to Success

Pressure and Support are Balanced

Rarely do a group of teachers spontaneously proclaim, "Let's work together to create pacing guides, write formative assessments, and analyze some data." As has been said many times before, the culture of teaching is isolated and entrepreneurial; sometimes teachers would just rather do it on their own. The decisions to begin, support, and maintain curriculum implementation processes often are made as a result of the pressure created by accountability demands, published test scores, and school district and school "report cards." In most cases the directive to align and implement curriculum is made at the district level and more rarely by the principal of an individual school. Many times such decisions are met with resistance, even when the process has been legitimized by school board action. We believe strongly in the procedures we have described for curriculum implementation, but we also feel that if the process *is* mandated, the rules of good leadership, communication, and support should be followed. That is, administrators need to remember, as Mildred McLaughlin suggests, that both pressure and support are required for successful implementation (1987). Implementation efforts that focus only on support without accountability inevitably waste resources. A balance of positive pressure and support is necessary.

We know that in any school, teachers are at many different levels of readiness to accept an innovation like the use of pacing guides. When the process of pacing guide development is introduced, most faculties will include teachers who will resist the effort, teachers who will be excited and enthusiastic, and teachers who will be willing to engage in the project, but confused about how to proceed. It is our belief that positive pressure and technical support can address the needs of teachers at different levels of acceptance.

In one of our local school divisions, the combination of positive pressure and technical support resulted in clear student achievement gains. After three years of low student performance on the state's high school social studies test, the high school principal issued a "call to action" to the social studies department. Strategies must be found, he said, to increase student performance on the state test. The administrators in this district were convinced that students were capable of higher achievement, and that the teachers were not only competent, but highly skilled at their jobs. After examining the teachers' course outlines, observing in their classrooms, and analyzing the state test results, administrators concluded that alignment of curriculum and instruction was indeed a problem. The principal placed a requirement on the department that they develop pacing guides for their classes that were correlated to the content on the state test. He also offered support and assistance in getting this work completed.

District-level instructional staff met with the social studies teachers regularly for a semester. During this time, support was offered in several forms. At department meetings, the format and process for developing pacing guides were presented. Materials offering detailed content from the state's adopted curriculum were provided, and help was offered, especially to new teachers, in interpreting this material. In follow-up meetings with small groups of teachers who all taught the same course, pacing guides were reviewed and discussed at various stages of their development. Clerical assistance was provided in typing and formatting the guides as they developed.

As might be expected, a few of the teachers did the work simply to comply with the principal's mandate. Others, as they began to see their pacing guide take shape, began to talk about how it influenced many of their instructional decisions. One teacher was prompted to examine his dependence on the (out-of-date) course textbook, which only roughly paralleled the state curriculum. As the year came to an end, teachers in the department described the process as a valuable one, but many remained unconvinced that they really had needed to do so much work to format their curriculum on paper.

That summer, the school underwent a construction project, which necessitated moving much of the furniture out of classrooms to other areas of the school. When teachers returned in August, a worried phone call was received at the district office from the department chair. The file cabinet where all the pacing guides had been stored for the summer was missing! The teachers were rushing to get their rooms organized and plan for the first weeks of school, and they had no time to waste! They needed those pacing guides, not only for themselves, but for two new teachers who had joined the department and had no idea where to begin.

The story has a happy ending. Because the district office had assisted with typing the pacing guides, back-up copies were safely stored on a file server. The teachers in this department, even those who were not happy about it, used the pacing guide process well and produced quality work. Because the work was high quality, it became a valuable resource to them, one they did not want to be without in starting off the school year. Finally, students' performance on the state end-of-course tests increased dramatically.

Pressure and Support from Central Office

As suggested by the preceding story, one of the sources for both pressure and support can be the central office. An expectation can be set, by the superintendent or assistant superintendent for instruction, for all schools to create pacing guides and set up a schoolwide process for assessing and monitoring student achievement. A reasonable timeline can be set, and central office personnel can be assigned to follow-up. A more likely (and more palatable) scenario is that the idea for using these processes is introduced and discussed at an administrative staff meeting or training session, which involves both principals and central office personnel. Consensus is achieved as to the need to engage in the processes, and the assistant superintendent negotiates the particulars with principals. Regardless, someone must take charge and say, "We're going to do this."

The district office can provide a variety of supports to the process:

- Training can be provided to principals and their leadership teams.

- Funds can be allocated to pay teacher stipends for summer work.

- Copies of the aligned curriculum, state guidelines and objectives, and other necessary materials can be provided to schools.

- Curriculum specialists can be assigned to assist where requested.

- Central office personnel can contact other districts to gather examples.

- Meetings across different schools can be organized to share and compare pacing guides.

- The testing supervisor can assist principals in organizing and presenting assessment data.

- The superintendent can ascend the bully pulpit to provide moral support.

As stated previously, we believe that the locus of control for this work should be the school, and that the district should serve only to motivate and support, not to direct. We feel certain that passive and active resistance can be minimized, diminished, and even eliminated when district administrators provide effective, timely, and appropriate support and avoid "being in charge." It can be very tempting for administrators, especially central office supervisors and others directly involved in curricular matters, to try to lead this effort; we feel strongly, however, that although these professionals are extremely important to the process, it is the line personnel—the school's teachers and principals—who hold the ultimate responsibility for the task, and thus should also control and direct it.

The Long-Term Goal is to Embed the Process into the School's Culture

As we mentioned in the first chapter, the process is not a "let's do it and get it over with" effort; it is important that throughout the process, school leaders realize that the goal is not to produce fancy pacing guides to make your school look good to the central office administrators who review them. The goal is to make these processes become part of the school culture. That is, using aligned curriculum, using data to make decisions, developing and using pacing guides, maintaining frequent and meaningful classroom and student assessment activities, holding staffing meetings, and accommodating students' needs should become central to how the school operates. One high school principal we know simply says, "It's how we do things around here, and everyone knows it." In fact, when she and her faculty members interview prospective new teachers, they ensure that candidates understand the school's focus on results and how pacing guides and staffing meetings work in their school. Near the end of her first year of teaching, one of these new teachers told us that she was certain that the reason for her very successful year was the fact that her colleagues and principal provided her with an aligned curriculum and helped her use pacing guides. Embedding the process in the culture does not happen overnight or by fiat, but we cannot overstress how important it is to make sure that these processes become a powerful part of the school's culture. It also must be remembered that embedding the process in a school's culture is something that takes place in the school, not in the central office.

Clearly Established Goals and a Time Frame for Completion are Prescribed

When beginning this process, it is important that all members of the school community, including support staff and parents, become well aware of what is to be accomplished and the established completion date. We worked with one school that sent (via email and printed newsletters) weekly updates as to the progress of pacing guide development to all staff members and parents. The front of the main office was decorated with a student's labeled drawing of a thermometer that indicated their progress. Regardless of the time frame you establish for completion, the goals of the process need to become part of the school's conversation.

Again, it is the responsibility of the central office administrators to provide supportive leadership along the way. If a school is having difficulties developing goals or time frames, central office support staff can perhaps provide examples, help eliminate snags or obstacles, and help communicate and facilitate activities between schools. Goals and the time frames for completing them should be unambiguous and observable, as the following examples illustrate:

- By November 15, each grade-level team will complete pacing guides in all core subjects for one nine-week grading period.

- By the end of the fall semester, each subject area team will have completed phase I pacing guides for their respective subjects.

All Work is Completed by Collaborative Groups

There are many advantages to making sure that the process of developing pacing guides does not become something completed in isolation from colleagues. That is, when formally established teams and work groups are assigned a particular task, the end result is nearly always better than when the tasks are completed by individuals working alone. To ensure investment in both the process and the final product it is the responsibility of the principal to facilitate the engagement of all faculty. Usually, teams are established based on common work groups; middle and high schools often simply use established departments or groups of teachers based on primary teaching assignments.

Elementary schools have a different challenge, because many elementary teachers teach all subjects. Because there is a need to have close articulation and connections across grade levels in each subject, many elementary schools have both grade-level teams and subject teams, each with clear goals and a time frame for task completion.

Communication Occurs Within and Among Schools

We believe that the process of creating and using pacing guides is a powerful tool for increasing student achievement. One of the major contributors to the effectiveness of this process is the increased and focused communication that occurs among teachers. To maximize the impact of the process, however, communication about curriculum and instructional pacing must go beyond the teaching team.

Within a school, sharing and discussing pacing guides across grade levels and departments can be a way of fine-tuning the instructional program. It is easier for students to learn (and remember what they've learned!) when teachers help them make connections among areas of study. In an elementary school, a fourth grade teacher who knows something about the content and pacing of the third grade curriculum can purposefully build on that curriculum. Better yet, if that fourth grade teacher knows which areas or skills have been the most difficult for children in third grade, then he can begin the year already understanding something about the learning needs of his students. This communication across grade levels can help to turn a program from a series of unconnected events (sixth grade, seventh grade, eighth grade, for example) into a cohesive, well-articulated program that makes sense to students.

Between schools, this same kind of grade-to-grade communication can ease the struggles associated with the transition from elementary to middle school and from middle to high school. Too often, we talk to teachers who seem to be mystified by the instructional program of the school that feeds into theirs. Sixth grade teachers, having met their new students, wonder why they seem so unprepared. Ninth grade teachers express frustration that students appear to have learned useless or trivial content, but not essential skills. At the same time, fifth and eighth grade teachers are working hard to prepare their students for success at the next level of schooling. Generally, these teachers tell us they have never shared their pacing guides with each other, and that conversations across schools about curriculum articulation are rare. The benefits of cross-grade discussion and planning, using pacing guides as a communication tool, can be a powerful factor in increasing student achievement.

In our experience, teachers have also found it helpful to exchange and discuss their pacing guides with other teachers of the same course or grade level at other schools. This can be difficult to arrange, but if the schools are within the same district, it is a productive use of a staff development day and can be coordinated with the help and support of division-level staff. This activity allows teachers who are teaching the same content, but in different schools, to compare and discuss the decisions they have made in designing their pacing guides. Sometimes, teachers discover that differences in their pacing guides exist because they are responding to the needs of different populations of students. Pacing guides also will look different, of course, in schools that have significant differences in their schedules or programs. The purpose of these cross-school discussions is not to make all the pacing guides alike. Rather, it is to exchange feedback with a colleague who is teaching the same or similar content, but in a different setting. We find that teachers often leave these conversations with new perspectives and valuable ideas.

Time is "Found" and Used Wisely

The process of aligning curriculum, developing pacing guides, and related activities such as attending staffing meetings and developing formative assessments do not need to add significant amounts of time to our already overburdened schedules if these activities replace something less worthwhile or something that can be completed in another way. One of the most important roles for the district's central office administration is to monitor and make sure the additional time for the work of alignment is provided and available.

There are no hard and fast rules or guidelines for how long the process takes. Some districts take the plunge into the deep end by having all teachers in every subject area complete pacing guides by a certain time. Others may choose to complete one subject at a time, completing a full set of all pacing guides for the entire K–12 system. For example, the district may wish to develop complete pacing guides for all mathematics curricula, from kindergarten through calculus, before beginning work on any other subject.

Momentum is Maintained

Used effectively, pacing guides will positively impact curriculum alignment and, in turn, student learning. The process we've described is effective. It is not, however, magic. It is straightforward and logical, but it is not quick or easy. The process works when it receives continued attention from teachers and administrators. In earlier chapters, we have encouraged principals to actively lead the process of pacing guide development, to fully participate in staffing meetings and other instructional discussions, and to offer whatever support and resources are available to assist teachers in the process. Teachers naturally take their cues about what's most important to do from their principals. Principals, both by their words and by their actions, set the tone for the pacing guide process in their schools. They must be persistent in providing time, resources, and training so that this work can occur. They must be confident in asking teachers to articulate and justify their pacing guide decisions. Perhaps most important, they must be unrelenting in their determination to keep the process on track and moving forward, even in the face of busy schedules, competing demands, and multiple priorities.

Different principals have very different leadership styles, of course, and not every principal will approach these challenges in the same way. Still, we believe that there are some keys to success in leading the process that contribute to its success:

- ◆ Keep the discussion focused on students and student needs.

- ◆ Keep asking questions about how teachers are using their pacing guides in their classrooms on a daily and weekly basis.

- ◆ When curriculum and instructional issues arise, ask yourself if the pacing guide might be a tool for helping you resolve these issues.

- ◆ Attend and participate in staffing meetings. If they are not happening, schedule them and be there.

- ◆ When you meet with teachers for supervision purposes, ask them to bring and discuss their pacing guide with you.

Both district administrators and school administrators can take significant roles in making sure motivation for alignment and monitoring remains high. Administrators can help teachers and principals avoid feeling like they are alone, unsupported or threatened by making regular visits to the schools, attending faculty meetings, meeting with parents, visiting classrooms, working with teachers as they develop pacing guides, and providing moral support. It is also important that these visits and actions be made in such a way that the focus is one of support, rather than threat or fear. Like most human beings, teachers who feel threatened will do little to take risks, will do little to give healthy input, and in general will do little more than the minimal required. When teachers feel truly supported in their endeavors and are provided the means to complete the tasks, the likelihood of success is immeasurably enhanced.

District specialists, both those responsible for the "core" academic areas, as well as exploratory or noncore areas, can play extremely positive roles in this process. One superintendent of a small rural school district asked all of his curriculum specialists to come up with at least one new resource a week for each school as they went through the process of developing pacing guides. This resulted in powerful cross-curricular communication and cooperation as specialists began to be seen as members of school teams rather than someone "from the office." It was not long before specialists from areas such as physical education and art began to help teachers find ways to connect these areas with the core academic areas.

As Kouzes and Posner suggest, celebrating successes can be a powerful mechanism to bring about needed changes in an organization's culture: "ceremonies … are the ingredients that crystallize personal commitment." (1987). The work that curriculum alignment entails is often very different from what we might think of as teachers' work, and yet this type of work needs to become part of the school and school district's culture. Central office administrators and curriculum specialists can enhance and support the opportunities for establishing it as part of the culture by providing not only fiscal or materials support but also by assisting with the celebration of teachers' successes.

Leadership Is the Key

The success or failure of the processes we have described in this book hinges on the leadership that is provided at both the school and district levels. Although many principals may be supportive of the process, often they are tentative in their leadership because they don't know exactly what to do. We find that in successful schools principals are active participants at all levels of the process: initiation; pacing guide design, review, and revision; assessment planning; staffing meetings; and data analysis and realignment. Figure 6.1 summarizes several actions principals can take to begin to embed this process into the school culture.

Figure 6.1. Leadership is Necessary for Pacing Guides to Work

Here's what principals can do

As teachers are working to develop their guides…

- Present the rationale (convincingly!).
- Set the expectation and plans for follow-up.
- *Participate in discussion; ask questions.*
- Coordinate a timetable for the work.
- Provide clerical or scheduling support if needed.
- Review guides and give meaningful feedback.
- Be the prime mover and coach for the project.

As you confer with individual teachers during the year…

- *Participate in discussion; ask questions.*
- Insist on real information about how students are doing.
- Provide assistance (perhaps from someone else!), and staff development as needed.

- Ask questions that cause teachers to justify what their pacing guides say.

- Be the prime mover and coach for the project.

As groups of teachers are working in pacing guide staffing meetings…

- Establish an ongoing conversation about learning.

- Provide data analysis related to their decisions.

- *Participate in discussion; ask questions.*

- Make resources available for intervention and differentiation.

- Insist that these meetings are focused and documented.

- Be flexible with scheduling, budget, and grouping to help students learn and achieve.

Similarly, central office administrators including the superintendent must search for ways to support this effort, beyond simply requiring it. Figure 6.2 summarizes a variety of actions that can be employed to encourage schools and principals to follow-through.

Figure 6.2. Leadership is Necessary for Pacing Guides to Work

Here's what central office administrators can do

As principals begin the process in their schools guides…

- Have the superintendent ascend the bully pulpit to provide motivation and support.

- Set expectations and plans for follow-up.

- Provide technical support.

- Provide monetary support.

- Provide time in the district calendar.

- Provide clerical or scheduling support if needed.

- Review guides and give meaningful feedback.

As you confer with principals and/or teachers during the year…

- Ask for copies of minutes of staffing meetings.

- Ask for real data about how students are doing.

- Continue to offer technical assistance and staff development as needed.

- Ask what changes in pacing, curriculum and/or assessment have been made as a result of staffing meetings.
- Discuss the provision of differentiation and instructional interventions.

As you review a school's progress at the end of the year...

- Establish an ongoing conversation focused on what principals can do to improve student learning.
- Provide data analysis of students' performance.
- Discuss plans for school-based data analysis.
- Discuss plans for pacing guide revision.
- Discuss plans and support for staff development.

We know that the development and use of pacing guides is a powerful process for aligning curriculum and assessment, as well as for analyzing and improving instruction. Like any initiative or school improvement strategy, however, the success of the process depends on active and effective leadership by district and school administrators. Every day, these leaders communicate their priorities through their actions.

Administrators tell us that high student achievement is their top priority and the central mission of their schools. Even so, we know that it is difficult to maintain a schoolwide focus on this mission in the midst of a multitude of day-to-day demands. In many cases, the biggest challenge is identifying a starting point and a strategy for attacking the challenge of improving student learning.

In this book, we have described a concrete, effective process for directly and strategically raising student achievement. If teachers are engaged and leaders are persistent, our design can provide both a starting point and a long-range strategy for schools engaged in this vital mission.

Appendix I

Elementary Pacing Guide Timetables

Development During a Two-Day Summer Workshop and Review and Revision During Faculty Meetings After the School Year Begins

Time Frame		Core Teachers	Specialty and Elective Teachers	Special Needs Teachers
Day 1	3 Hours	Mathematics Guide	Kindergarten Specialty Guide Grade 1 Specialty Guide	Assigned to Core Team
	3 Hours	Science Guide	Grade 2 Specialty Guide Grade 3 Specialty Guide	Assigned to Core Team
Day 2	3 Hours	Social Studies Guide	Grade 4 Specialty Guide Grade 5 Specialty Guide	Assigned to Core Team
	3 Hours	Language Arts Guide		Assigned to Core Team

Faculty Meetings After School Begins

Session 1	2 Hours	Review Lower Grade Core Guides	Review K–1 Core Guides	Assigned to Core Team
Session 2	2 Hours	Review Higher Grade Core Guides	Review 2–3 Core Guides	Assigned to Core Team
Session 3	2 Hours	Review Specialty Area Guides	Review 4–5 Core Guides	Assigned to Core Team
Session 4	2 Hours	Revise LA and SS Guides	Revise K-2 Specialty Guides	Assigned to Core Team
Session 5	2 Hours	Revise Math and SC Guides	Revise 3–5 Specialty Guides	Assigned to Core Team

Development, Review, and Revision During Faculty Meetings After the School Year Begins

	Time Frame	Core Teachers	Specialty and Elective Teachers	Special Needs Teachers
Session 1	2 Hours	Mathematics Guide	Kindergarten Specialty Guide Grade 1 Specialty Guide	Assigned to Core Team
Session 2	2 Hours	Science Guide	Grade 2 Specialty Guide Grade 3 Specialty Guide	Assigned to Core Team
Session 3	2 Hours	Social Studies Guide	Grade 4 Specialty Guide Grade 5 Specialty Guide	Assigned to Core Team
Session 4	2 Hours	Language Arts Guide		Assigned to Core Team
Session 5	2 Hours	Review Lower Grade Core Guides	Review K-1 Core Guides	Assigned to Core Team
Session 6	2 Hours	Review Higher Grade Core Guides	Review 2–3 Core Guides	Assigned to Core Team
Session 7	2 Hours	Review Specialty Area Guides	Review 4–5 Core Guides	Assigned to Core Team
Session 8	2 Hours	Revise LA and SS Guides	Revise K-2 Specialty Guides	Assigned to Core Team
Session 9	2 Hours	Revise Math and SC Guides	Revise 3–5 Specialty Guides	Assigned to Core Team

Appendix II

Secondary Pacing Guide Timetables

Development, Review and Revision
During a Five-Day Summer Workshop

Time Frame		Core Teachers	Elective Teachers	Special Needs Teachers
Day 1	3 Hours	Core Course 1 Guide	Elective Course 1 Guide	Assigned to Core Team
	3 Hours	Core Course 2 Guide	Elective Course 2 Guide	Assigned to Core Team
Day 2	3 Hours	Core Course 3 Guide	Elective Course 3 Guide	Assigned to Core Team
	3 Hours	Core Course 4 Guide	Elective Course 4 Guide	Assigned to Core Team
Day 3	3 Hours	Review lower sequential core course guides	Review lower sequential elective course guides	Assigned to Core Team
	3 Hours	Review higher sequential core course guides	Review higher sequential elective course guides	Assigned to Core Team
Day 4	2–3 Hours	Review related elective course guides	Review related core and elective course guides	Assigned to Core Team
	3–4 Hours	Revise core guides	Revise elective course guides	Assigned to Core Team
Day 5	6 Hours	Polish and publish	Polish and publish	Assigned to Core Team

Development, Review, and Revision During Faculty Meetings After the School Year Begins

Time Frame		Core Teachers	Elective Teachers	Special Needs Teachers
Session 1	2 Hours	Core Course 1 Guide	Elective Course 1 Guide	Assigned to Core Team
Session 2	2 Hours	Core Course 2 Guide	Elective Course 2 Guide	Assigned to Core Team
Session 3	2 Hours	Core Course 3 Guide	Elective Course 3 Guide	Assigned to Core Team
Session 4	2 Hours	Core Course 4 Guide	Elective Course 4 Guide	Assigned to Core Team
Session 5	2 Hours	Review lower sequential core course guides	Review lower sequential elective course guides	Assigned to Core Team
Session 6	2 Hours	Review higher sequential core course guides	Review higher sequential elective course guides	Assigned to Core Team
Session 7	2 Hours	Review related elective course guides	Review related core and elective course guides	Assigned to Core Team
Session 8	2 Hours	Revise Core Course 1 & 2 Guides	Revise Elective Course 1 & 2 Guides	Assigned to Core Team
Session 9	2 Hours	Revise Core Course 3 & 4 Guides	Revise Elective Course 3 & 4 Guides	Assigned to Core Team

Appendix III

Social Studies & Science—Grade 1: Sample Pacing Guide

Social Studies & Science—Grade 1: Pacing Guide

Subject/Grade Level: Social Studies, Science/Grade 1[*]

Communities		August 26–September 20
	Objectives/Essential Understandings & Skills	*Essential Knowledge*
1.	The student will recognize that communities include people who have diverse ethnic origins, customs, and traditions, who make contributions to their communities, and who are united as Americans by common principles.	Communities include people of different ethnic origins who come from different places around the world. Citizens make valuable contributions to their communities.
2.	The student will interpret information presented in picture time lines to show sequence of events and will distinguish between past and present. Make timelines that include ♦ family events ♦ school events ♦ local community history	

---

* Adapted from the VA Standards of Learning by teachers at William Perry Elementary School.

Social Studies & Science—Grade 1: Pacing Guide

Subject/Grade Level: Social Studies, Science/Grade 1

Seasons, Precipitation, and Temperature		September 22–*
	Objectives/Essential Understandings & Skills	*Essential Knowledge*
3.	◆ Identify types of precipitation as rain, snow, and ice (sleet, hail) and the temperature conditions that result in each one. ◆ Relate a temperature and precipitation chart to the corresponding season (daily or weekly). ◆ Measure and chart changes in plants, including budding, growth, wilting, and losing leaves. ◆ Predict how an outdoor plant would change through the seasons. ◆ Compare and contrast the four seasons of spring, summer, fall (autumn) and winter in terms of temperature, light, and precipitation. ◆ Compare and contrast the activities of some common animals (e.g., squirrels, chipmunks, butterflies, bees, ants, bats, and frogs) during summer and winter by describing changes in their behaviors and body covering. ◆ Comprehend the concepts of hibernation, migration, and habitat, and describe how these relate to seasonal changes. It may be useful to recognize common Virginia animals that hibernate and migrate, but specific names of animals is not the focus of student learning here. ◆ Infer from people's dress, recreational activities, and work activities what the season is.	**Earth Patterns, Cycles, and Change** Calendar, Fall begins, Johnny Appleseed Seasonal changes and their affects on ◆ plants (growth, budding, falling leaves, wilting), ◆ animals (behaviors, hibernation, migration, body covering, habitat), and ◆ people (dress, recreation, work).

Social Studies & Science—Grade 1: Pacing Guide

Subject/Grade Level: Social Studies, Science/Grade 1

Columbus Day		October 8
	Objectives/Essential Understandings & Skills	*Essential Knowledge*
4.	**Holidays** The student will discuss the lives of people associated with Presidents' Day, Columbus Day, and the events of Independence Day (Fourth of July).	

Maps		October
	Objectives/Essential Understandings & Skills	*Essential Knowledge*
5.	The student will (a) Recognize basic map symbols, including references to land, water, cities, and roads (b) Use cardinal directions on maps (c) Identify the physical shape of the United States on a map.	**Terms to know** ♦ Map: A drawing that shows what places look like from above and where they are located ♦ Globe: A round model of the Earth ♦ Symbol: A picture or thing that stands for something else ♦ Cardinal directions: The directions of north, east, south, west **Map symbols to identify** ♦ Land ♦ Water ♦ Cities ♦ Roads The terms north, east, south, and west are used to determine location on simple maps.

Social Studies & Science—Grade 1: Pacing Guide

Subject/Grade Level: Social Studies, Science/Grade 1

Scientific Investigation, Reasoning, and Logic		October
	Objectives/Essential Understandings & Skills	*Essential Knowledge*
6.	Through exploration and investigation, students will: ♦ Conduct observations using the senses and simple instruments to enhance observations ♦ Classify objects or events according to attributes or properties ♦ Communicate observations orally and with simple graphs, pictures, written statements, and numbers ♦ Measure length, mass, and volume ♦ Predictions are based on patterns of observation rather than random guesses	

Maps and Symbols		November
	Objectives/Essential Understandings & Skills	*Essential Knowledge*
7.	The student will construct a simple map of a familiar area, using basic map symbols in the map legend	

Social Studies & Science—Grade 1: Pacing Guide

Subject/Grade Level: Social Studies, Science/Grade 1

Force, Motion, and Energy		November and December
	Objectives/Essential Understandings & Skills	*Essential Knowledge*
8.	The student will investigate and understand that moving objects exhibit different kinds of motion. ♦ Make and communicate observations about moving objects. ♦ Predict an object's movement using its size, shape, and the force of the push or pull on it. ♦ Describe and classify the motion of an object as straight, circular, curved, or back and forth. ♦ Understand that vibrations may create sound, such as humming, strumming a guitar, plucking a rubber band. ♦ Compare the movement of objects using graphs, pictures, and/or numbers.	♦ Objects may have straight, circular, and back and forth motions. ♦ Objects vibrate. ♦ Pushes or pulls can change the movement of an object. ♦ The motion of objects may be observed in toys and in playground activities.

Appendix IV

English 9:
Sample Pacing Guide

English 9: Pacing Guide

Subject/Grade Level: English 9*

Short Story & Nonfiction	August 26–September 30
Objectives/Essential Understandings & Skills	*Essential Knowledge*
◆ Complete culminating activities for Summer Reading Project. ◆ Present a 3–5 minute oral presentation. ◆ Review familiar and introduce new literary terms. ◆ Read short works of non-fiction and fiction. ◆ Introduce expository writing process. ◆ Complete at least one 5 paragraph essay. ◆ Map out the parts of a short story: exposition, rising action, climax, falling action, resolution. ◆ Review basic elements of grammar within the context of reading literature and writing papers. ◆ Learn new vocabulary as it is presented in the reading materials.	**Students are expected to master:** **Oral Presentations:** ◆ Use examples from their knowledge and experience to support the main ideas of their oral presentations. ◆ Respond clearly and informatively to audience questions about their oral presentations. **Read and Analyze Literature:** ◆ Explain the relationship between an author's style and literary effect. ◆ Explain the influence of historical context on the form, style, and point of view of a literary work by discussing how the subject matter, form, style, literary type, theme, and purpose of the work reflect the culture and events of the times in which it was written. (On occasion, an author's works may influence historical events.) ◆ Describe the use of images and sounds to elicit the reader's emotions. ◆ Analyze an author's use of language to depict sound. ◆ Analyze the techniques used by the author to convey information about a character, such as direct exposition, character's actions, character's thoughts.

(Short Story & Nonfiction continues on the next page.)

---

* Thanks to Leah Kirkpatrick for the use of her pacing guide.

Short Story & Nonfiction *(continued)*		August 26–September 30
	Objectives/Essential Understandings & Skills	*Essential Knowledge*
		◆ Analyze a character's development throughout the text, including: dynamic, flat, static, and round characters; caricatures; and stereotypes.
		◆ Analyze an author's use of diction to convey ideas and content, such as rhetorical questioning, connotation, denotation, pun, understatement.
		◆ Analyze an author's use of structuring techniques to present literary content, such as: foreshadowing, flashback, plot, setting, theme, protagonist, antagonist, foil, point of view, speaker, narrator.
		Writing Skills:
		◆ Use prewriting strategies and organize their writing.
		◆ Communicate clearly the purpose of the writing.
		◆ Write clear, varied sentences.Use specific vocabulary and information.
		◆ Arrange paragraphs into a logical progression.
		◆ Revise their writing for clarity.
		◆ Develop written products that demonstrate their understanding of composing, written expression, and usage/mechanics
		◆ Edit final copies of their writing for correct use of language, spelling, punctuation, and capitalization.

English 9: Pacing Guide

Subject/Grade Level: English 9

The Odyssey	October 1–November 6
Objectives/Essential Understandings & Skills	*Essential Knowledge*
Learn about epic poetry and oral traditions in literature. **Read the *Odyssey*:** ♦ Identify, define, and understand new literary terms. ♦ Create poetry or narrative writing in response to reading. ♦ *Odyssey* projects–these can be oral presentations of written or visual projects that deal with Greek society, narrative and oral tradition in literature or deeper scholarship on the *Odyssey*. ♦ Watch the *Odyssey* film.	**Oral Presentations:** ♦ Use relevant details, such as facts, statistics, quotations, information from interviews and surveys, and pertinent information discovered during research, to support the main ideas of their oral presentations. ♦ Use examples from their knowledge and experience to support the main ideas of their oral presentations. ♦ Cite information sources by giving credit in their oral presentations to authors, researchers, and interviewers. ♦ Respond clearly and informatively to audience questions about their oral presentations.

English 9: Pacing Guide

Subject/Grade Level: English 9

Expository (Process) Writing/Narrative Writing	November 7–December 3
Objectives/Essential Understandings & Skills	*Essential Knowledge*
♦ Read and analyze practical or technical print materials. ♦ Go over how to write a clear expository paper after reading examples of good expository writing. ♦ Have students write a paper or give an oral presentation which teaches/explains a process. ♦ Read and analyze short works of fiction. ♦ Go over new literary terms. ♦ Read a short story that demonstrated clearly narrative writing. ♦ Write a narrative essay.	**Oral expository presentation option:** ♦ Define technical and specialized language to help the audience understand the content. ♦ Use relevant details to support the main ideas of their oral presentations. ♦ Use examples from their knowledge and experience to support the main ideas. ♦ Cite information sources by giving credit in their oral presentations to authors, researchers, and interviewers. ♦ Respond clearly to audience questions. **When writing expository and narrative papers, students are expected to:** ♦ Use prewriting strategies and organize their writing. ♦ Communicate clearly the purpose of the writing. ♦ Write clear, varied sentences. ♦ Use specific vocabulary and information. ♦ Arrange paragraphs into a logical progression. ♦ Revise their writing for clarity. ♦ Develop written products that demonstrate their understanding of composing, written expression, and usage/mechanics.

(Expository (Process) Writing/Narrative Writing continues on the next page.)

Expository (Process) Writing/Narrative Writing *(continued)*		November 7–December 3
	Objectives/Essential Understandings & Skills	*Essential Knowledge*
		◆ Edit final copies of their writing for correct use of language, spelling, punctuation, and capitalization.
		◆ Identify a hypothesis and the supporting details in a scientific report.
		◆ Evaluate the clarity and accuracy of information found in informational and technical texts.
		◆ Synthesize information from sources and apply the information in both written and oral presentations.
		◆ Generate questions for discussion, further reading, and research after reading a selection.
		◆ Extend general specialized vocabulary through reading and writing. Employ activities that support a process for reading.
		◆ Read instructions and successfully apply the information acquired in order to use computer software, assemble or construct models or equipment, or complete a project.

English 9: Pacing Guide

Subject/Grade Level: English 9

Poetry Unit		December 4–January 18
	Objectives/Essential Understandings & Skills	*Essential Knowledge*
	◆ Read a variety of poetry from a large span of time periods, cultures, and literary movements. ◆ Identify poetic and literary elements in poems. ◆ Learn about famous poets.Write original poetry. ◆ Listen to poetry being performed.Read poetry out loud.	**In Poetry, students are expected to:** ◆ Explain the relationship between an author's style and literary effect. ◆ Explain the influence of historical context on the form, style, and point of view of a literary work by discussing how the subject matter, form, style, and point of view of a literary work by discussing how the subject matter, form style, literary type, theme, and purpose of the work reflect the culture and events of the times in which it was written. (On occasion, an author's works may influence historical events.) ◆ Describe the use of images and sounds to elicit the reader's emotions. ◆ Analyze and author's sue of language to depict sound. ◆ Analyze an author's use of structuring techniques to present literary content, such as verse, stanza, couplet, hyperbole ◆ Analyze an author's use of figurative language (words and phrases) to create images, such as metaphor, simile, analogy, symbolism, paradox, oxymoron, apostrophe, allusion, imagery.

English 9: Pacing Guide

Subject/Grade Level: English 9

Research Paper		January 20–February 28
	Objectives/Essential Understandings & Skills	*Essential Knowledge*
	◆ Research a topic using a variety of print and electronic resources. ◆ Write a research paper on a selected topic. ◆ Create an MLA-formatted bibliography for the research paper.	**In Research, students are expected to:** ◆ Define plagiarism. ◆ Recognize that citing sources correctly is key even when paraphrasing. ◆ Use quotation marks when quoting exactly. ◆ Understand the consequences. ◆ Distinguish original ideas from those borrowed from others. ◆ Distinguish common knowledge from information demanding credit. ◆ Use MLA documentation. **In using electronic databases, students are expected to:** ◆ Identify and use key terms, such as electronic database, search engine, electronic mail, World Wide Web, Web browser, on-line services, hotlinks, narrow the focus of a search, identify useful search terms, scan evaluate, and select resources based upon reliability, accuracy, and relevance to the purpose of the research select appropriate databases, evaluate the quality of Internet sources.

English 9: Pacing Guide

Subject/Grade Level: English 9

Romeo and Juliet		March 1–April 10
	Objectives/Essential Understandings & Skills	*Essential Knowledge*
	◆ Read *Romeo and Juliet*. ◆ Learn about Elizabethan theater through research. ◆ Identify poetic and literary terms in *Romeo and Juliet*. ◆ Perform scenes and monologues from *Romeo and Juliet*. ◆ Compare selections from the old and new *Romeo and Juliet* films. ◆ Demonstrate understanding of *Romeo and Juliet* through a written test, paper, or presentation. ◆ Attend a play at the Black Friar's Playhouse, Staunton, Virginia.	◆ Participate in dialogue scenes from plays. ◆ Use verbal and nonverbal techniques for the presentation, such as: appropriate tone, diction, articulation, clarity, type and rate of delivery, and the use of pauses for emphasis ◆ .Nonverbal techniques include but are not limited to eye contact, facial expressions, gestures, and stance. ◆ Analyze and critique the relationship among the purpose, audience. ◆ Evaluate the impact of the presentations by critiquing the effectiveness of the speaker's demeanor, voice, language, gestures, clarity of thought, organization of evidence, relevance of information, and delivery. ◆ Evaluate the effectiveness of verbal and nonverbal techniques in presentations. In writing, students will meet the requirements set forth in earlier units for structure and content, while adding new knowledge and dramatic literature.

(Romeo and Juliet continues on the next page.)

Romeo and Juliet (continued)			March 1–April 10
	Objectives/Essential Understandings & Skills		*Essential Knowledge*
			Theater: Students are expected to identify the two basic parts of drama:
			◆ Staging–lighting design and cues, costumes, set design, set decoration: properties/props stage movement/ blocking; voice: tone, pitch, inflection, emotion, facial expressions, make up, curtain cues, music/ sound effects
			◆ Scripting–dramatic structure: exposition, rising action, complication, conflict, climax, falling action, resolution, denouement, dialect, monologue, soliloquy, dialogue, aside
			Students will also:
			◆ Compare and contrast the elements of character, setting, and plot
			◆ Describe how stage directions help us understand a play's setting, mood, characters, plot, and theme
			In reading literature, students are expected to analyze an author's use of structuring techniques to present literary content, such as aside, soliloquy, foil.

English 9: Pacing Guide

Subject/Grade Level: English 9

Concluding Literature Unit	April 12–May 30
Objectives/Essential Understandings & Skills	*Essential Knowledge*
◆ Read a play that contains stage directions and other conventions of modern theater. ◆ Identify and discuss aspects of drama. ◆ Perform selected scenes from the play. ◆ Read short stories. ◆ Respond to and analyze performances by classmates in writing.	Students are expected to: ◆ Choose an appropriate poem, monologue, short story, or play for individual or group performance. ◆ Participate in dialogue scenes from plays, dramatic readings from short stories and/or novels, and performance interpretations of poetry. ◆ Analyze and critique the relationship among the purpose, audience, and content of presentations. ◆ Use prewriting strategies. ◆ Communicate clearly the purpose. ◆ Write clear, varied sentences. ◆ Use specific vocabulary and information. ◆ Arrange paragraphs logically. ◆ Revise their writing for clarity. ◆ Develop written products that demonstrate their understanding of composing, written expression, and usage/mechanics. ◆ Edit final copies of their writing for correct use of language, spelling, punctuation, and capitalization.

Appendix V

Algebra 1:
Sample Pacing Guide

Algebra 1: Pacing Guide
Phase I: Curriculum Planning*

Course: Algebra 1   Year: 2001–02

Time Frame	Unit Title	Content and Skills	Vocabulary
8/26–8/27	Variables & Expressions	The student will demonstrate the ability to translate verbal expression into mathematical expressions and vice versa.	Variables Algebraic expressions Factors Product Power, base, & exponent Sequence, term, pattern
8/28–8/29	Patterns & Sequences	The student will extend patterns and sequences.	
8/30 & 9/2	Order of Operations	The student will evaluate expressions containing real numbers. [Quiz here]	Order of operations
9/3–9/4	Stem & Leaf Plots	The student will display & interpret data.	Data, statistics, stem, & leaf plot
9/5	Open sentences	The student will solve open sentences by performing arithmetic operations.[Quiz here]	Open sentence Solving open sentence Solution Replacement sets
9/6 & 9/9	Review and help dayIdentity & Equality Properties	The student will recognize & use properties.	Element Solution set Equations Inequality

---

*   Thanks to Zane Pierce of Waynesboro City Schools.

Time Frame	Unit Title	Content and Skills	Vocabulary
9/10–9/11	Distributive Property	The student will simplify expressions and evaluate expressions.	Additive identity Multiplicative identity Multiplicative inverse Reciprocal Reflexive Property Symmetric Property Transitive Property Substitution property
9/12–9/13	Commutative & Associative Property	The student will sketch and interpret graphs in addition to simplifying and evaluating expressions. [Quiz here]	Term, like terms, equivalent expressions Simplest form Coefficient
9/16	Review and help day. (Chapter 1)		Commutative Property Associative Property
9/17–9/18	Preview of graphs and functions.		Functions Vertical & horizontal axes Ordered pairs Origin Independent variable Quantity Dependent variable Relation Domain & Range
9/18	Chapter Test		
9/19–9/20	Integers & The Number Line	The student will state coordinate of point, graph integers, and add integers on number line.	Number line Whole numbers Negative number Integers Venn Diagram Graph Coordinate

Time Frame	Unit Title	Content and Skills	Vocabulary
9/23	Integration: Statistics: Line Plot	The student will interpret numerical data from a table display and interpret statistical data on a line plot.	Line Plot
9/24	Add & Subtract Integers	The student will find absolute value and add & subtract integers. [Quiz here]	Absolute value Matrix Discrete mathematics
9/25	Rational numbers	The student will compare and order rationals and find numbers between two rational numbers.	Cross product Unit price Density property
9/26	Add & Subtract Rational numbersDistributive Property	The student will add & subtract rational numbers and simplify expressions that contain rationals.	Matrix
9/27 &9/30	Multiply rationals	The student will multiply rationals and use scalar multiplication of matrices.	Scalar multiplication
10/1	Divide rationals	The student will divide rationales. [Quiz here]	Complex fractions
10/2	Square roots and real numbers	The student will find square roots, classify numbers, and graph solutions of inequalities on a number line.	Square root Perfect square Radical sign Principal square root Irrational numbers Real numbers Completeness property

Time Frame	Unit Title	Content and Skills	Vocabulary
10/3	Problem Solving: Equations and formulas	The student will explore problem situations and translate verbal sentences and problems into equations or formulas and vice versa using the four step problem solving method.	Defining the variable Problem solving plan Formula
10/4	Chapter Test		
End of First 6 Weeks			
10/7	Solve Equations with Add & Subtract	The student will solve equations with addition and subtraction.	Addition Property of Equality Equivalent Equation Solve and equation Subtraction Property of Equality
10/8	Solve Equations with Multiplication & Division	The student will solve equations with multiplication and division	Multiplication Property of Equality Division Property of Equality
10/9	Solve Multistep equations	The student will solve equations involving more than one operation and by working backwards. [Quiz here]	Working backwards Multistep equations Consecutive integers Number theory
10/10	Integration: Geometry: Angles & Triangles	The student will find supplement and complement of an angle and find the measure of third angle of triangle.	Supplementary angle Complementary angle Triangle Equilateral triangle Congruent
10/11 & 10/14	Solve equations with variables on both sides	The student will solve equations with variables on both sides and solve equations containing grouping symbols.[Quiz here]	Isosceles triangle Right triangle Obtuse triangle Acute triangle

Time Frame	Unit Title	Content and Skills	Vocabulary
10/15–10/16	Solve equations and formulas	The student will solve equations and formulas for a specified value.	
10/17	Review and help day		
10/18	Chapter Test		
10/21	Ratios and Proportions	The student will solve proportions.	Ratio, Proportion Extremes and means Rate
10/22	Similar triangles	The student will find unknown measures of sides of similar triangles.[Quiz here]	Similar Corresponding sides & angles
10/23	Percents	The student will solve percent problems and problems involving simple interest.	Percent, percentage Base, rate, simple interest
10/24	Direct and Inverse Variation	The student will solve problems involving direct and inverse variation.	Direct & inverse variation Constant of variation
10/25	Chapter Test		
10/29	The Coordinate Plane	The student will graph ordered pairs on a coordinate plane and solve problems by making a table.	Axis, Origin X-axis, Y-axis Quadrant Coordinate planex-coordinate, y-coordinate Graph
10/30	Relations	The student will identify domain, range and inverse, and show relations as sets of ordered pairs, tables, mappings, and graphs.	Domain, Range, Inverse Mapping Relation
10/31	Equations & Relations	The student will determine range for a given domain and graph solution sets.	Equation in two variables

Time Frame	Unit Title	Content and Skills	Vocabulary
11/1	Review Day		
11/4–11/5	Graphing linear relations, functions and equations.	The student will graph linear equations. [Quiz here]	Linear equations Standard form (Ax+By=C) Slope intercept form (y=mx+b)
11/6–11/7	Functions Quiz C	The student will determine whether a given function is a relation and find a value of a function for a given value of the domain.	Function Functional notation Vertical line test
11/8 & 11/11	Write equations from patterns	Write equations to represent relations given some of the solutions for the equations.	
11/12–11/13	Measures of variationReview	The student will calculate and interpret range, quartile, inter-quartile range, lower & upper quartiles.	Measures of variation Range Quartile Lower & Upper quartile Inter-quartile range Outlier Box-and-whisker plot
11/14	Chapter Test		
End of Second 6 Weeks			
11/15	Slope	The student will find the slope of a line given coordinates of two points on the line.	Slope Rise, run Slope formula (m=rise/run)

Time Frame	Unit Title	Content and Skills	Vocabulary
11/18–11/21	Write linear equation in point-slope and standard form	The student will write linear equations in point-slope form and in standard form.	Point-slope formula $(y-y1)=m(x-x1)$ Slope of a Vertical line Slope of a Horizontal line Standard form $(Ax+By=C)$ Shortcuts for slope & y-intercept: Slope $= -A/B$ y-intercept $= C/B$
11/22 & 11/25–11/26	Statistics: Scatter plot and best fit lines	The student will graph and interpret points on a scatter plot, draw and write equations for best fit lines, and make predictions by using equations. [Quiz here]	Scatter plots Model Positive correlation Negative correlation Regression lines (use calculator)
12/2	Write linear equations in slope intercept form	The student will solve problems by using models, determine the x & y-intercepts of linear graphs from their equations, write equations in slope intercept form, and write and solve direct variation equations.	
12/3–12/4	Graph linear equations	The student will graph a line given any linear equation, graph linear equations to show trends, and graph a line by ordered pairs, intercepts, and slope intercept forms.	y-intercept x-intercept Slope intercept form: $y=mx+b$

Time Frame	Unit Title	Content and Skills	Vocabulary
12/5	Integration: GeometryParallel & Perpendicular Lines	The student will determine whether two lines are parallel or perpendicular by slope and write equations of lines that pass through a given point parallel or perpendicular to the graph of a give equation.	Parallel lines Perpendicular lines Parallelogram
12/10	Review		
12/11–12/12	Chapter Test		
12/13	Solve Inequalities by Addition and Subtraction	The student will solve inequalities by addition and subtraction.	Set builder notation Functional notation
12/16	Solve Inequalities by Multiplication and Division	The student will solve inequalities by multiplication and division.	
12/17–12/18	Solve Multistep Inequalities	The student will solve multistep linear inequalities when replacement values are given and solve linear inequalities involving more than one operation.	
12/19	Quiz		
12/20 & 1/6	Solve Compound Inequalities	The student will solve problems by making a diagram and solve compound inequalities and graph their solution sets and solve problems that involve compound inequalities.	Compound inequality Diagram Intersection Union

Time Frame	Unit Title	Content and Skills	Vocabulary
1/7	Integration: Statistics: Box-and-whisker plots	The student will display and interpret data on a box-and-whisker plot.	Box-and-whisker plot Extreme values Quartile Inter-quartile range Lower & Upper quartile 1st & 3rd quartile Outliers (use calculator)
1/8	Chapter Test		
End of Third 6 Weeks			
1/9–1/10	Graph Systems of Equations	The student will solve systems of equations by graphing and determine whether a system of equation has one solution, no solution or infinitely many solutions by graphing.	System of equations Intersecting Parallel Coinciding Inconsistent & consistent Independent Dependent
1/13–1/14	Substitution	The student will solve systems of equations by using substitution method and organize data to solve problems.	Substitution
1/15	Elimination by adding and subtracting. Solving systems.	The student will solve systems of equations by using the elimination method with addition and subtraction.	Uniform motion Word problems Mixture word problems
1/16–1/17	Elimination using multiplication and division Quiz B	The student will solve systems of equations by using the elimination method with multiplication and division and determine the best method for solving systems of equations.	

Time Frame	Unit Title	Content and Skills	Vocabulary
1/20	Chapter 8	The student will demonstrate competency of material through completion of a test.	
1/21–1/23	Multiply monomials Quiz A (critical)	The student will multiply monomials, simplify expressions involving powers of monomials, and solve problems by looking for a pattern.	Monomial Constant Product of powers Power of a power Power of a product Power of a monomials
1/24 & 1/27–1/28	Divide monomials Quiz B	The student will simplify expressions involving quotients of monomials and negative exponents.	Quotient of powers Zero exponent Negative exponent
1/29	Scientific notation	The student will express numbers in scientific and standard notation and find products and quotients of numbers expressed in scientific notation.	Scientific notation
1/30	Polynomials Quiz C	Find the degree of a polynomial. Arrange terms of a polynomial in ascending and descending order.	Polynomial Monomial, binomial, trinomial Degree of a term Degree of a polynomial Ascending order Descending order
1/31–2/3	Add and subtract polynomials	Add and subtract polynomials.	
2/4–2/5	Multiply a polynomial by a monomialQuiz D	Multiply a polynomial by a monomial. Simplify expressions involving polynomials.	

Time Frame	Unit Title	Content and Skills	Vocabulary
2/6–2/7 & 2/10	Multiply polynomials Quiz E	Use the FOIL method to multiply two binomials. Multiply any two polynomials by using the distributive property.	FOIL method
2/11–2/13	Special products Quiz F	Use patterns to find $(a+b)^2$, $(a-b)^2$, $(a+b)(a-b)$	Square of a sum Square of a difference Difference of squares
2/14	Chapter 9	The student will demonstrate competency of material through completion of a test.	
End of Fourth 6 Weeks			
2/17–2/18	Factor and Greatest Common Factors	The student will find prime factorization of integers and GCF for sets of monomials.	Prime numbers Composite numbers Prime factorization Unique factorization theorem Factored form Greatest Common Factor
2/19–2/21 & 2/24	Factors using Distributive Property Quiz A (reloop if necess)	Students will use the GCF and distributive to factor polynomials, and use grouping techniques to factor polynomials with four or more terms.	Factoring by grouping
2/25–2/28	Factor trinomials Quiz B (reloop if necess)	The student will solve problems by using guess and check and factor quadratic trinomials.	Guess and check method. Prime polynomial.

Time Frame	Unit Title	Content and Skills	Vocabulary
3/3–3/4	Factor differences of squaresQuiz C	The student will identify and factor binomials that are the differences of squares (product of a sum and difference).	Pythagorean triple
3/5–3/6	Perfect squares and factoring Quiz D	The student will identify and factor perfect square trinomials.	Perfect square trinomials
3/7 & 3/10–3/12	Solve equations by factoring Quiz E	The student will use the Zero Product property to solve equations.	Zero Product Property
3/13–3/14	Chapter 10	The student will demonstrate competency of material through completion of a test.	
3/17–3/20	Graph quadratic functions	The student will find the equation of axis of symmetry and the coordinates of the vertex of a parabola and graph quadratic functions.	Quadratic function Parabola Vertex Maximum, minimum Axis of symmetry
3/21 & 3/24	Solve quadratic equations by graphing Quiz A	The student will use estimation to find roots of a quadratic equation and find roots of a quadratic equation by graphing.	Quadratic equations Roots Zeros of the quadratic function
3/25–3/28	Solve quadratic equations by using Quadratic formula Quiz B	The student will solve quadratic equations by using the quadratic formula.	Quadratic formula
3/29–3/30	Chapter 11	The student will demonstrate competency of material through completion of a test.	
3/31–4/1	Integration: GeometryThe Pythagorean Theorem	The student will use the Pythagorean theorem to solve problems.	Pythagorean Theorem $a^2 + b^2 = c^2$

Time Frame	Unit Title	Content and Skills	Vocabulary
4/2–4/3	Simplifying Radical Expressions	The student will simplify square roots and radical expressions.	Radicand Product Property of Square Roots Quotient Property of Square Roots Simplest Radical Form
End of Fifth 6 Weeks **TEST**			
	Chapter 12		

References

Canady, R. L., & Rettig, M. D. (1995). *Block scheduling: A catalyst for change in high schools.* Princeton, NJ: Eye on Education.

Craft, M. (2002, December 10). Lessons tailored to fit the learner, not vice versa. Seattle Times.

English, F. W. (1980). Curriculum mapping. *Educational Leadership, 37*(7), 558–559.

Friend, M., & Cook, L. (1996). *Interactions: Collaboration Skills for School Professionals.* White Plains, N.Y: Longman Publishers.

Hayes-Jacobs, H. (1997). *Mapping the big picture: Integrating curriculum and assessment K-12.* Alexandria, VA: Association for Supervision and Curriculum Development.

Hitchcock, C., Meyer, A., Rose, D., & Jackson, R. (2002). Providing new access to the general curriculum: Universal design for learning. *Teaching Exceptional Children,* Nov/Dec, p. 8–17.

Janney, R., & Snell, M. E. (2000). *Teachers' guides to inclusive practices: Modifying schoolwork.* Baltimore, MD: Paul H. Brookes Publishing.

Kame'enui, E. J., & Simmons, D.C. (1999). *Toward successful inclusion of students with disabilities: The architecture of instruction.* Reston, VA: Council for Exceptional Children (CEC).

Kouzes, J. M., & Posner, B. Z. (1987). *The leadership challenge: How to get extraordinary things done in organizations.* San Francisco: Jossey-Bass.

Marzano, R. J. (2003). *What works in schools: Translating research into action.* Alexandria, VA: Association for Supervision and Curriculum Development.

Marzano, R. J. (2000). *A quantitative synthesis of research on school-level, teacher-level, and student-level variables related to academic achievement.* Aurora, CO: Mid-continent Research for Education and Learning.

McLaughlin, M. W. (1987). Learning from experience: Lessons from policy implementation. *Educational Evaluation and Policy Analysis, 9*(2), 171–178.

Minskoff, E. H.., & Allsopp, D. H. (2003). *Academic success strategies for adolescents with learning disabilities and ADHD.* Baltimore, MD: Paul H. Brookes Publishing.

Orkwis, R., & McLane, K. (1998). *A curriculum every student can use: Design principles for student access.* Reston, VA: ERIC/OSEP Special Project, Council for Exceptional Children.

Polloway, E. A., & Patton, J. R. (1993). *Strategies for teaching learners with special needs* (5th edition). New York: Merrill.

Rettig, M. D., & Canady, R. L. (2000). *Scheduling strategies for middle schools.* Larchmont, NY: Eye On Education.

Rettig, M. D., & Canady, R. L. (1998). High failure rates in required mathematics courses: Can a modified block schedule be part of the cure? *NASSP Bulletin, 82*(596), 56–65.

Torrance, E. P., & Sisk, D. A. (1999). *Gifted and talented children in the regular classroom.* Buffalo, NY: Creative Education Foundation Press.

United States Department of Education (1999). *To assure the free and appropriate education of all children with disabilities (Individuals with Disabilities Education Act* (21st Annual Report to Congress on the Implementation of the Individuals with Disabilities Education Act). Washington, DC: Author.